dynamics
of
stillness

This edition published in 2019 by
Eddison Books Limited
www.eddisonbooks.com

Text copyright © Ian Wright 2019
Design copyright © Eddison Books Limited 2019
Cover design by Paul Palmer-Edwards

British Library Cataloguing-in-Publication data available on request.

ISBN 978-1-85906-447-4

1 3 5 7 9 10 8 6 4 2

Printed in Europe

dynamics
of
stillness

Develop your
senses and reconnect
with nature through
meditation

IAN WRIGHT

Eddison Books Ltd

CONTENTS

Introduction 6

$\mathscr{I}$NTRODUCTION

This book is offering something genuinely new and different. It is based on a course I have been teaching for more than ten years, the Dynamics of Stillness. It is different from a normal meditation practice in that meditation is not the main purpose of what we are doing. The dynamics of stillness process takes us step-by-step through a series of practices, which are designed to first bring our nervous system to a state of quiet neutral, an important step which allows us to deepen any meditative practice that follows. From this point, we explore and develop our relationship to our own health and our relationship to the natural rhythms and tides in nature. Everything in nature has a fluid consistency and tides are rhythms within this fluid nature. Our course work allows us to attune our sense to these tides. With each practice, we deepen our connection to the great stillness, which is ever present in and around us always. If we can learn to take our awareness back to a place where we feel stillness, which the Taoists would term returning to the source of everything, this place of stillness holds the potential for everything. There is a great dynamic within this stillness, which can be reached once we are in a state of neutral.

The course is based on over thirty practices and is about developing a specific skill base, a combination of mindful meditation and sensory development with each technique building on the last. In part one, we start with finding the state of neutral where we learn to quiet our minds – a vital prerequisite to this course – and from there we learn about tempo, presence and tuning our senses to the great stillness, which is ever present. We learn about attention and how to become consciously aware of where we place it and how to place it anywhere. Then, we begin to develop our sensory awareness to 'sense' fluid fields both in ourselves and in nature.

In part two, we learn detailed practices to deepen our connection to nature, to learn how to feel the great tides within it as well as its alchemical processes. These techniques also help us to understand aboriginal practices and 'the story on the wind'.

In part three, we learn how to meet our health and learn the techniques needed to self-heal. We then deepen our practice to find wholeness and oneness within ourselves. This process helps us become aware of how we use, and how to repattern, our senses as we work towards developing a holistic 'felt-sense' – a term coined by American psychologist Eugene Gendin and now widely used to describe a feeling sense in or around the body that if we focus on, can bring insight.

The Dynamics of Stillness course was developed to share important practices with people from all walks of life, to encourage the learning of techniques to open up sensory awareness and to start relating to, and finding potential health within, ourselves. Rather than focusing on what feels wrong within our bodies, learning to shift our perception onto what feels well, and healthy, will change our relationship to our health. As we progress through the course, we deepen our self-acceptance and learn to let our attention be moved by the moment to a proliferating stillness and, eventually, to a dynamic stillness.

I wish you well, and hope you enjoy these practices.

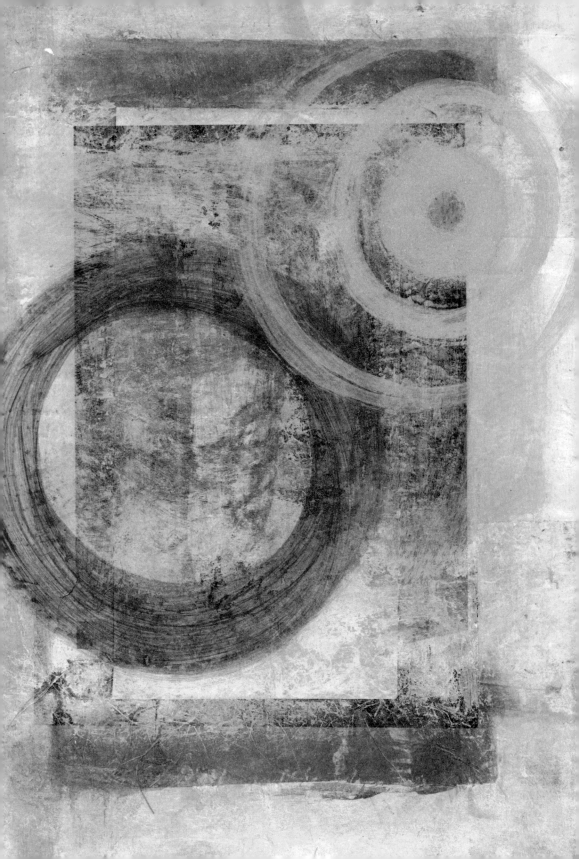

SECTION

I

THE STATE
of NEUTRAL

CHAPTER 1

FINDING OUR NEUTRAL

It is amazing how much chatter goes on in our brains. Every waking second we are processing information. From the moment we get up in the morning, we are thinking about something: What am I doing today? What shall I wear? What shall I eat? Alongside these day-to-day thoughts, there are undercurrents of deeper murmurings: Why am I unhappy? Is this job right? Am I in the right relationship? Is my child OK at school? Different aspects of ourselves vie for attention; our ego talks to us, perhaps saying, 'I really deserve better'. Our emotions raise their heads in subtle ways through grief, fear, anger and guilt.

With all these thoughts going on at the same time, it is amazing we function at all. Our only respite is when we are listening to music, watching television, talking or some other form of sensory excitement. These activities can be relaxing, connecting, calming and even meditative, but they can also be a distraction from important aspects of our lives. This world of information overload bombards us. Advertising, for example, can be designed to appeal to our ego and to our emotional vulnerabilities. Its intention can be to trigger an emotional response in us; for example, saying if you eat this, or do this, you will have the perfect body and be happy. This also implies that we cannot be happy without the product that the advertiser is pushing us to buy.

One consequence of this information overload is that we can feel unhappy, empty and confused. We then find that we need to develop strategies for coping with these uncomfortable feelings. Some strategies like watching television and drinking alcohol distract us but can lead to more unhealthy feelings and physical sensations. However, it is also possible to choose to seek out healthier patterns of behaviour to satisfy our deeper selves.

Sleep should provide us with rest and relaxation. But with our senses being overstimulated, our sleep is often disturbed. Our nervous systems cannot wind down enough to get to sleep – when our nervous systems do not get the chance to settle into a quiet place, how can we fall into a natural sleep? And even if we do, we can wake soon after, thinking and worrying again.

But maybe we need to address the underlying issues with sleep difficulties and find a method which, when practised daily, can improve this dynamic and start to offer a sense of peace, tranquillity and connection.

There are age-old techniques designed to help us improve the quality of our lives, including prayer, meditation, yoga and taking exercise. But how often do we enter these with a quiet mind? Through these techniques, we may occasionally find a moment's peace – thankfully – but we usually still bring along chatter. Our thinking mind comes in. Before we can potentially enter this world of stillness, peace and inspiration, we need to find the right place to start. We need to learn to be able to take our minds out of gear, to find our 'neutral'.

Our neutral is a state that can be likened to taking the car out of gear. Our minds tend to be driving us ever onwards to the next destination – thinking, thinking, always driving and striving onwards. In neutral, our mind relaxes its grip, albeit temporarily. We take it out of gear and we start to relax.

This relaxation provides the groundwork for deeper practices to flourish.

It is interesting to note that children are often naturally in this neutral state. It is a beautiful innate state, where they are in the moment and free to act spontaneously and without judgement. They seem to be undistracted and they can act and react instinctively, free of consideration for anything but themselves and their current experiences.

This state of being in neutral tends to slowly diminish as we enter our early teens: the hormones kick in, social pressure mounts and our internal judge appears. At the same time as we begin to become self-aware, this natural state of being starts to wane. During this time, when we begin to compare ourselves to our peer group and to media figures – never feeling quite good enough and with the sense of needing to find our place in the world – we react to this feeling of inadequacy and of trying to find our way, and the natural spontaneous neutral seems to slowly go. As we grow from childhood to adulthood, our reasoning capabilities become a more dominant requirement to satisfy social norms. As such, it seems that the more we use our brains to reason, the less we can find a quiet, neutral way of being.

Being in a neutral state has an interesting effect on our nervous systems, and can avoid triggering a state of high alert as when the sympathetic nervous system deals with survival responses: the flight, fight, fright responses. These responses ready our body for action, releasing chemicals like adrenaline to allow fast responses. Unfortunately, we live a lot of our lives in this state of reactivity, mostly where no threat is present. This keeps our bodies in a low-level state of anxiety for too much of the time.

Over time, this has a direct effect on several of our body systems. This heightened state of stimulation can lead to an increase in pulse rate and blood pressure, and it can constrict the capillary beds. The effect of this is to decrease the blood supply to our organs and body and put a strain on our cardiovascular systems.

This overstimulation directly affects our ability to sleep. We need our brains to be in neutral to sleep and adrenaline prevents this. You remember those times when you had something important to do the next day or were worrying about something? It is so hard to switch off and get to sleep. Again, we are reminded of the natural ability of children, who usually find it so easy to get to sleep wherever they lay their heads at the end of a tiring, active day. As we get older, that simple switch-off process becomes harder. We tend to wind down slowly over a few hours and wait until we are almost dropping off to try to sleep. Or we take to medications or alcohol to help us relax. Actively taking our brains out of gear could significantly help our ability both to get to sleep and to improve our sleep quality.

Let's start to see if we can take our nervous systems out of gear and find some degree of neutral. This neutral state is a vital prerequisite for all later techniques.

Finding Your Neutral

Begin the practice

This core practice will be one to which you return to throught this course. You can be sitting in nature, lying in bed, riding a train or a plane, or even walking or running. But to start with, try this practice sitting comfortably in a chair, feet on the ground, spine quite straight but not tense. Feel the bones of your bottom on the chair; allow yourself to feel the weight of your body on the chair.

Let your head be upright but let go of any tension in the neck, just let it soften in your mind; let your chest have the sense of being wide; let your eyes relax, feel the eyeball soften; let your hands sit comfortably in your lap.

Keep your eyes open but let your vision be nonspecific, just relaxed, or – if this is hard – gently close them. Now just let go of your awareness.

Become aware of chatter

The first thing to realize is that there is all this chatter going on and to wake up to that. An age-old Buddhist technique for effective meditation is to become aware of the noise in your head but to do nothing about it, to become like an impartial observer, adding a healthy sprinkle of compassion for yourself: not to judge it, nor try to control or stop it in any way. Awareness is a huge step – to observe this chatter with no judgement.

Maintain awareness of the quiet behind the chatter

Next, do something important, namely not to try to stop the noise. You must actively allow it, letting your mind wander into the past, the future, onto thoughts, ideas, places, people, worries, fears, anticipations, whatever – but you must also do something very important, which is to maintain awareness of the quiet behind the chatter.

There are many techniques to achieve this. My favourite is one you can do in loud environments, or even on the train or in a meeting. It is also excellent if you are finding it difficult to get to sleep:

Bring your attention gently onto your breathing, but notice something delicate and soft there – this is not deep breathing, it is quite shallow breathing. As soon as you turn your awareness to this delicacy in the breath, the usual response from your body/mind is for a million thoughts to demand your attention. Now, really allow these thoughts, never suppress them, but all the while bring your attention back to the softness in your breathing. Even if you are in great pain, you can try to treat it like noise and allow the feeling of the pain. All the while, keep bringing your attention back to something that feels soft or gentle in your breathing.

I have taught this technique to hundreds of children and adults and it has been a very helpful exercise to develop. It is hard to do at the beginning, but with a little practice you can start to maintain it for a few minutes. If you can do this, you tend to find a sense of quietness comes in. Often people report a warm feeling in their chest and they start to gain the feeling of some peace.

Don't try to hold onto any peaceful feeling, just quietly observe it coming and going. Maintain your concentration on the delicacy in your breathing, the quiet, sweet softness of your breath. Just do this for three to four minutes at first, then return to it later. The ability to concentrate on this softness builds as you practise. Your sense of neutral is when your brain switches down a gear, just for a minute or two at the beginning. It will become easier and quieter with practice.

This is harder to do when stressed, but if you are persistent, it can calm those feelings of stress and anxiety.

Practise this technique as much as you can – ideally, once or twice a day

This technique is simple, but it is very effective. It not only starts to bring you to your neutral point, but also refocuses your attention from feeling what is wrong in your body to what feels well, gentle and delicate – an expression of your health – which is a huge step.

Over a period of days and weeks, you will retrain your mind/body into starting to feel neutral, which can bring peace. You will even start to find yourself slipping into neutral without trying. This is only the beginning. You will build many layers of technique from here and each stage is vital in the practice.

Conclusion

You have introduced the idea of bringing a little quiet neutral to your racing mind and senses. This is the beginning of your practice. Keep trying this technique even if you find it hard at first. The secret is to completely accept any feeling or sensation that arises in you, even if that feeling is one of being deeply anxious – it's OK, let it be. From here, you will develop your practice in the coming chapters.

CHAPTER 2

ACCEPTING, ALLOWING AND OBSERVING

We have started on the path to develop a meditative practice that, if we can just work on it a little daily, even for ten minutes, I hope will soon start to bring real, palpable benefits. These benefits will come in our sense of neutral peace, our ability to cope with stress, and our deepening connection to the energy fields and natural tides in our body, and to nature as a whole.

In the first practice, we started to bring our attention to the noise, internally and externally, and began to actively bring our awareness to the softness in our breathing. But usually, as soon as we begin this process – as soon as we sit down and start to quieten our minds to look towards finding a degree of neutral – we are bombarded with a whole plethora of thoughts, feelings and sensations.

Thoughts are the usual story – worries such as what's for dinner? I must pay that bill, and so on. Feelings are slightly deeper and can be sadness, happiness or, perhaps, anger. Sensations are feelings in our body – comfort or, more often, discomfort. They can also be little aches and pains and niggles that we all have. This is entirely normal. It happens to everyone, even seasoned meditators and teachers.

There is a way to move past these thoughts, feelings and sensations. Our normal response is to try to push them away, judge them or react to them, especially emotions. The way through this, to change this response, is to do the opposite: to not react, but to accept, allow and eventually just observe these thoughts, feelings and sensations.

If we realize that these thoughts and sensations are impermanent – meaning that they come and they go – and we must just wait, they will pass, like clouds across a clear blue sky. What happens for us is that a thought, or a movement of the mind or body occurs, and we react to it. From that reaction, we continue with a sequence of reactions. These reactions can go on and on, and as we continue our minds get cloudy and agitated. This is life! The amazing trick here is that if we learn not to react to these thoughts or feelings or sensations, the sequence of reactions will gradually slow down and even stop, and our mental sky can become clear and crystalline blue.

So, how do we stop these reactions of the mind?

ACCEPT

The first step is to accept that everyone in the world has thoughts, feelings and sensations – it is part of being alive and human. Accepting this fact gives us a little break from our eternal self-judgement. We can be so hard on ourselves, especially when trying to sit and find a little peace within. Just trying to accept this – that it is OK to have thoughts and sensations – gives us a small window of self-acceptance to build on.

ALLOW

The second step on this path is to allow your own thoughts and sensations to arise – let them come. The very action of allowing changes our dynamic to them and has an effect of softening their impact as opposed to reacting to them, which seems to harden them. What tends to happen here is that the more we allow, the deeper the thoughts, emotions and sensations are that arise. It is as if the mind is saying, 'Hey! Listen to me!'

So just keep allowing these thoughts, emotions and sensations to arise. They may be anything from, 'My leg is sore,' to 'I'm hungry,' to 'I forgot I had to pay that bill today,' on and on, to deeper feelings of sadness and old grief. Whatever it is, just allow it, but do not indulge it: let the feeling, emotion or sensation come.

What is amazing is that even deep pain and grief, if it comes up and you fully allow it – without any reaction to it – will soften and start to pass; even that deep emotion is impermanent. Do not let your mind attach and react. Just let it come, allow it, and it will soften and start to pass. It can be helpful to see these sensations as clouds across a perfect blue sky, gently but continually moving in and out of your awareness.

OBSERVE

From this important standpoint of accepting and allowing you will gradually come to a point of simply observing these thoughts and sensations, of becoming totally impartial to them without indulging or reacting.

This change of approach takes time and practice. I have been applying this practice for more than twenty years and I still find it a challenge. The point is, if we allow and accept the fact that we will never perfect this and can only gradually get better at it, it gives our internal judge the day off.

It's good to start applying these techniques whenever we become present to our thoughts, emotions and sensations, whether sitting down to practise these exercises, in front of an angry boss or with an irritable child.

This process of accepting and allowing will become incredibly freeing. If practised daily, it can become a part of your interaction with life, which may, alone, bring peace.

In my work as an osteopath, I spend much of my day working with children and tiny babies. Often the babies are extremely irritable, in distress from colic or reflux, for example. As I approach them, I apply these three techniques – that of accepting, allowing and observing. This means that my body starts to relax, which in turn can help the baby to relax. It is a simple but very effective technique to apply to many different situations.

Buddhists talk of our human suffering as impermanent and have a variety of methods to overcome these thoughts, feelings and emotions. Some techniques will encourage the practitioner to say, 'Thinking, thinking', whenever these thoughts, feelings and emotions come up. Others look at focusing on differing aspects of the breath.

For me, just the process of accepting, allowing and observing gives me the opportunity to encourage a deeper process within myself. Let's try to put this into practice.

Accepting, Allowing and Observing

Begin the practice

Find a quiet, comfortable spot to spend a few minutes. Get comfortable and allow yourself to feel your back against the chair and your bottom on the seat. Just enjoy the sensation of your weight being held up by the chair.

Sit quietly and bring your attention to your breathing. More importantly, find something delicate and soft in your breath. It could take a few minutes for your breath to soften and sweeten. As you start to relax, your breath will quieten a little.

From here, you will very quickly start to become flooded with the usual thoughts, emotions or sensations. First, reassure yourself that this is good – this is part of the process. Just sit with them.

Allow this feeling

What starts to happen is that one sensation will become the clearest. It may be a thought or a sensation or even an emotion. From here you are going to do something – you are going to fully allow this feeling. If it helps, say, 'I fully allow this feeling.'

As you really allow it, watch this feeling take its natural course. It may become stronger – allow that. It may soften – allow that too. More likely, it will be replaced by another emotion or perhaps an even deeper feeling.

This will probably go on through eight to ten different emotions or feelings or thoughts. Keep allowing the feeling, and just try to start to observe them – observe their coming and going. Maybe see them as clouds across the perfect blue sky of your mind. What may happen is that everything goes quiet, even for a few seconds, and then the thoughts will start again. Remember that quiet moment, that sense of the clear blue sky in the mind.

Glimpse the quietness

Such feelings and thoughts or body sensations can at times feel intense. The important thing to realize is that these feelings are just trying to move, to shift from being locked in you. Continue to allow them, just let them be, and try to glimpse the quietness, the blue sky, behind them. That quietness is you and the thoughts, feelings and sensations are simply over-laying patterns.

Conclusion

With practice, these quiet moments will increase, but it's important not to let your mind think this. Just accept what is happening right now and don't think about goals or achievements. All you are doing is allowing and observing.

This process can be challenging at first. Take your time, do a few moments here and there, and come back to it. Eventually, the process will allow you to move through feelings, emotions and sensations in a manageable way.

If you are really stressed, however, or if you have a history of emotional trauma, it is much harder to achieve this – it can feel too much. In this case, it is important to get support. When faced with trauma and the anxiety that springs from it, you need a team of support. This includes your GP, a psychotherapist or counsellor and a trusted friend or family member. If you feel overwhelmed at any stage, seek support, then once this is in place, carry on slowly and gently.

It may also feel overwhelming if you suffer from chronic physical pain. When you start to sit quietly and practise allowing, accepting and observing, the pain can initially feel too strong. If this happens to you, complete this process little by little, just practising for a few minutes a day. I have often seen these techniques work with patients of mine who are in severe chronic pain.

The point is to take it slowly and gently and not force things.

CHAPTER 3

TIMING AND TEMPO

TIMING

There is something about perfect timing, isn't there? When we get the feeling that we are in the right place at the right time and everything falls into place. How rare are those moments?

Timing is key in many things, most obviously in sport. When a tennis shot is timed perfectly, it can be unstoppable. Similarly, when we perfectly time what we are going to say in a conversation, it can have the intended impact. If we say what we want to at the key moment, it almost makes for a deeper connection with the person, but if we say it too early or even too late, it simply won't do that.

Great actors and comedians seem to have this perfect timing, knowing just when to give that extra half-second pause that engages us. But it seems very hit-and-miss as to whether we can achieve perfect timing, due to great skill, great luck or a combination of both.

As our skills improve, say, in a sport, it becomes less a matter of luck to hit the perfect shot. That's why practice makes our timing better and better. The same is true of public speaking. The more we do it, the better we get and the more well-timed our responses are. What is practice, though? Really, practice is simply paying attention to what we are doing and repeating the activity again and again.

But what about other elements in life that seem more like luck? How can we achieve better timing and so maximize our potential in life?

We repeat actions a lot but often without perfect timing; we make mistakes again and again and still do not learn. How can we make our timing more in sync with the movement of the universe? If we could do this, everything would flow a little better.

In sports and other activities, we have identified two elements that, gradually, bring better timing. Paying attention to what we are doing and repeating the action – both elements together constitute practice. So how can we practise at life? We spend enough time repeating activities, but one thing that we often forget to do is to pay attention to what we are doing.

TEMPO

There is another element that could lead us to have better general timing in life and this is the idea of learning to read and to start living in tempo with the natural rhythm of life. What is it to be in rhythm and in tempo with life? This is something we learn by starting to sense the natural flow of things, the natural way they unfold, and just going with it. Not trying to speed up or slow down the natural order, but to just flow with it. This is hard to do, especially if things are going in a way that doesn't suit us. It's like swimming in a river that is flowing down towards the sea. If we swim upstream it is hard going, but if we flow down with the river, we hardly need any energy. The river has a natural tempo, a natural rhythm and to be in tempo with life, we need to do a few things.

Firstly, as I've said, we need to pay attention to what we are doing. But more than that, we need to start to become more aware of our environment, of people and what they are saying when they are talking, and of what is happening in and around us, including in nature. To do this, we need to learn to sense the world around us.

We all have wonderful senses – sight, hearing, touch, smell, and an awareness of where our bodies are in space and time – and all too often we take these for granted. The best way to engage our senses is to become fully aware of them in our environment.

Explore vision first; bring your awareness to what is in your direct line of vision and what is in the distance. Really become aware of what you are seeing in the moment. It's amazing how much we filter through our eyes, how much we can actually see. Our brain only processes a tiny proportion of what we see, that which it considers important in the moment. It applies a series of filters to our vision and if it didn't do this, we would be in a state of feeling constantly overwhelmed.

The question is, though, how do we decide what is important and what is not? We learn this over our lifetime. As our vision starts to wake up when we are still babies, we learn to focus our attention on important objects: Mum, food, drink and the things we need to be concerned about in our environment. We learn very quickly to filter out those things we deem unimportant.

As we grow, our visual priorities change with our developing consciousness. We learn to pay attention to other factors, such as our living environments and finding potential mates. Our senses are driven by quite basic human requirements. If we think about indigenous hunters or trappers, they learn over the years to see what we don't – for example, the tiny changes in the environment that indicate a recent animal passage. They learn to pay attention to those almost invisible varying elements.

From here, just spend a moment with our hearing. Take in all the sounds, near and far. Isn't it amazing how much we screen out of what we see and hear, feel and smell? As before, with our vision, we must screen a lot of what our senses are telling us from moment to moment in order not to feel overwhelmed.

It is clever how our brains, if our attention is somewhere else, just put most of what we sense into the background. We are only alerted when something new is noticed, which sends a fresh signal to the brain and wakes up our attention to the moment. My attention right now is on what I'm writing, but if I stop, I can hear early-morning spring birdsong, an incredibly beautiful sound. So now, I'm trying to write and listen, which slows me down and enlivens the writing process.

For me to be in tempo with life, I have to slow down to this natural pace. This is a place where my senses are moved by the moment – that change in light as the sun rises, that change in birdsong right now. An amazing thing happens when I start to be in tempo with life through nature. It feels as though my brain softens, my need to finish this chapter falls away, and I relax and start to enjoy the moment.

When this happens, I really slow down and relax, and don't want to type. I could easily just sit here, hearing, feeling and seeing nature, and becoming aware of the deep stillness behind it. In this place, all is well. I always feel safe, held by life, and I have no drive to do anything. It's a beautiful place and one can really see from here how the German-born spiritual teacher Eckhart Tolle could sit on a park bench in London for two whole years, quite content.

It seems that to get into tempo with things, an important access point is to become aware of our senses and to pay attention to our environment. This immediately takes us out of the world of abstract thinking to something more real.

This process can slow us down, but it can also do the opposite. Nature isn't necessarily slow, it can be very rapid, while also being unhindered by thinking. Animals don't think about something – they act in the moment, their senses totally awake and aware. If we tune into our senses and open our awareness, we have more chance of acting in tempo with life. Let's start to explore these ideas in the following practice.

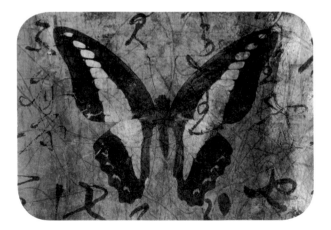

Timing and Tempo

Through this practice, you will start to learn to develop your senses and your sensory awareness. This will hopefully connect you more deeply with nature, with yourself and with others.

Begin the practice

For this practice, you do not need to sit and it can even be done while walking to work.

Bring attention to your vision

Start by bringing your attention to your vision. What can you see directly in front of you, right now? Don't move your head or eyes. Just see what is beyond the book or screen you are looking at.

Now take in your surroundings for a second, see the colours, shapes and objects around you, and see your horizon. Enjoy all the different colours and shapes of things. Do not think about anything you see, just look and do not judge, simply enjoy the looking. It's quite nice, isn't it?

Bring awareness to your hearing

What is the landscape of sound around you now? What is in the background? It's amazing how many background sounds you filter out. I often find that even in a busy city,

the sounds of nature are still there behind the noise. But don't filter out the noises you don't like, just allow your awareness to take them in without judging them. See if you can hear a quieter humming behind the noises, almost a stillness behind the sounds. Really enjoy these sounds and let them in, unfiltered, by thinking about them.

Bring awareness to your touch

Now spend a second feeling the floor under your feet, or the chair under your bottom. Can you feel the sense of the book you are holding or the device you are looking at: how do they feel? The process here is to expand the normal sense of touch, of feeling the physicality of an object, and developing it further to a feeling sense.

Your 'nature-sense'

As you spend a few minutes on these simple ways to explore your vision, hearing and touch, what may happen is that your thinking brain can start to quieten. Maybe, just for a moment, you are in the present. You are not in the land of concepts or thinking of the future or past but right here, breathing softly and aware of your environment.

Now, open your awareness to all of these senses at once. You can call this sensory awareness 'nature-sense'. It is tricky at first, so you may only do it for a second or so, but keep trying.

Your 'felt-sense'

Once you can spend a few seconds trying to feel nature-sense, what I want you to sense is if there is a tempo to it, a natural rhythm. Just ask the question and be open to the answer. What I mean by tempo is that if you really open your senses to the environment, can you start to feel some notion of coherence between all these sounds, sights and senses? Is there a quality that can link them, maybe some underlying quietness beneath all these sensations connecting yourself and all of them? I don't want you to think about this, just try to feel it. Let's call it your 'felt-sense'.

Conclusion

If you are finding this difficult, don't worry, you are at the beginning. You are starting to change the way your senses interact with your brain. This sensing is beyond conceptual thinking – it's like feeling life through nature. It can be difficult to begin with, but you can do it eventually.

Finding this rhythm may start you on the path to greater timing and tempo, but you need to practise and to slowly awaken your senses. In the history of the world, many ancient aboriginal tribes have been documented as being able to use their senses in extraordinary ways. So maybe this nature-sense is something through which you can start to deepen your own sensory awareness. Perhaps these ancient practices are within your ancestral aboriginal collective memory with which you can reconnect.

You will be developing these ideas and, hopefully, your felt-sense as you go on.

CHAPTER 4

THE GIFT OF THE PRESENT

Young children playing is such a beautiful sight. They seem to have no agenda and are unfettered by what society says, or how they should act and be in the world. Their attention is solely on what they are doing. It doesn't matter if they are playing in a beautiful garden or in the street. They are inquisitive, free and totally in the moment. How often do we as adults take time to play, to just be in the moment, to laugh freely and to have some fun?

As we start to understand what our neutral point is, a natural consequence is that we are brought more into the present. Our mind still wanders to the future and the past, but more time is spent in the here and now. In this state, time can feel like it is slowing down. As a consequence, we begin to get a sense that we have more time for things. How does that work?

FUTURE AND PAST UNIVERSES

It seems we spend much of our waking time in future or past universes, thinking and planning different potential scenarios or analyzing what has happened. Was it good or good enough? Did we upset someone? Sometimes we feel regret or anger about the past, or fear for the future. If we really look at this, it seems such a waste of time.

Of course, we must plan our day; of course, we must review the past – otherwise how would we learn from it? Of course, we should remember beautiful memories of love and those sweet moments in life, but living in these places doesn't allow for the beauty of the moment. I like the phrases 'Take time to smell the roses' and 'Wake up and smell the coffee.' They bring to mind the idea of being in the present moment.

The danger for us is that if we spend all our time in future planning or past analysis, we don't spend enough time in the present moment, spontaneous and free to be – to be playful, to observe, to let our senses breathe and to sense life.

There is a garden at one of my practices that takes my breath away with its sheer beauty. However, people often pass through and don't even see it. With our minds either in the future or the past, we can actually miss out on the incredible and beautiful things that are happening right now.

Isn't technology wonderful? A huge number of us own a smartphone, which means that we have access to a vast amount of information, worldwide, at the touch of a button. I am amazed at how quickly we can research almost anything. The danger is, though, that we can all too easily get lost in this world of information and sensory stimulation.

I love technology and the world it has opened up for me, but I must police the use of it, by myself and by my three teenagers. We have had dinners where all four of us are playing with our mobile phones so now they are banned from the table unless there is something specific that we want to research to aid our conversation.

SIT STILL AND BE

How wonderful it is just to sit and be: to stop, to have no agenda, even for a few moments, to smell the roses, look at the sky, feel the softness of our breath, hear the wind, watch the leaves – or even observe a plane cruising above us.

Usually, the only time we are brought into the present moment is when we are in sharp distress. As we have discussed, in an emergency, our bodies respond by releasing a variety of hormones, including adrenaline and cortisol. Our nervous systems wake up and we are on full alert, our senses more acute and alive, our adrenaline pumping. We smell, hear and see more acutely and our hearts beat faster, ready for action.

SUPER-AWARENESS

In this way, we – and most animals – have adapted to deal with perceived threats. It works because our super-awareness alerts us to dangers. For animals, it is awareness of predators; for us, it is awareness of dangerous situations. In these moments, with our senses alive and alert, we are brought directly into the present so we can respond to the danger. This is a vital instinct deep within our bodily functions, governed by the more primitive parts of the brain in the brainstem. Of course, the problem in modern life of overstimulation to the senses means that our systems are on full alert. The strange thing with this is that we are not brought into the moment – quite the opposite, we are deeply distracted. This is confusing for the mind and body.

LIVE IN THE PRESENT

Here, in the Dynamics of Stillness training, we are going to start to untangle this body/mind mix-up, which will serve to calm this response. It will allow us to start living more in the present and eventually to centre ourselves in stillness.

Even at key moments in life, sometimes it can be really hard to remain present and take in the full beauty of those precious times. How wonderful – and deeply calming – would it be to live in the moment, even for a few minutes each day? How wonderful to just be in the moment, to feel our breath and be moved by life with all its wonder, pain and beauty?

Sitting in the Present

If you can spend just five minutes a day retraining your brain to be in the moment, it can bring many rewards. As you go back to normal life, you find that spontaneously you can be brought back to the present moment by your senses, and this is a wonderful feeling. Those roses really start to smell great, those children playing can distract you, and maybe the mental chatter of thoughts, feelings and sensations can quieten, just a little bit, and allow your brain to quietly breathe.

Begin the practice

Build on what you have been practising. In a way, you are learning to retrain your brain and senses to achieve deep stillness.

Be in the present

Try now to take a few minutes to sit and really be in the present. It helps if you can concentrate on the softness of your breathing, building on what you have already practised. Making your breath soft can be done in two ways. The first is meeting something that feels soft and delicate within your breath. The second is consciously breathing gently, softening and taking in smaller breaths. You can do this even if you have difficulty in breathing or if you suffer from anxiety. Breathe softly, not deeply, and allow your outbreath to be slightly longer than your inbreath. You have plenty of air!

Let your thoughts come and go

It can be helpful to see them as clouds across a beautiful blue sky – the sky being your mind and the clouds being your thoughts, whether grey thunder clouds or white wispy clouds, whether they come or they go. Behind these clouds, the sky is still there and always will be. What is this blue sky? The blue sky behind the thoughts, feelings and sensations is you. And this has a stillness to it.

Once you feel the internal thoughts and noises begin to quieten, allow your mind to take in your surroundings. Start with the sounds, whether they are loud and irritating – even if there is the loud banging of a power tool outside, or heavy traffic, or if they are the songbirds in full voice. It doesn't matter. Listen without judging any of these sounds; simply allow them to arise and then to fall away.

Notice your surroundings

Let your view move unhindered – do not control it, let it move wherever it wants to. Maybe now, let your eyes wander to the minute detail of the crumb on the floor, or to the vista and faraway horizon. Just let your vision be moved by the moment.

Next, start to bring awareness to your sense of smell. Mostly, you do not use this sense except when brand new aromas come into your consciousness. Common, everyday smells fade into the background just as everyday sounds do. When you bring awareness to your sense of smell, everyday smells are treated by the brain as something new, different and important.

Conclusion

Finally, spend a few minutes feeling things in your immediate environment. Pick up an object and enjoy its texture and contours. If you are near water, whether a stream or a kitchen sink full of water, spend a few minutes feeling the water by moving your hands through it and enjoying the texture, temperature and fluidity.

Take time to enjoy all your senses. Let them direct what they want to do, whether you are drawn to a sight, smell, sound or texture. Allow your mind to be in this present moment and let yourself be moved by it. Whatever it brings up, just observe, allow and accept. Now close your eyes, sit in the quiet of the moment and just be.

CHAPTER 5

DEVELOPING A PRACTICE

In the two great traditions of spiritual practice that are Buddhism and Taoism (or Daoism), teachers over many generations have talked about the idea of letting go of attachments and desires. Attachments are what link us to the past, be it attachment to relationships, power or money. Desires are all about the future, our future wishes and dreams. Attachment and desire both keep us in either the past or the future.

ON THE PATH TO LETTING GO

Many times I have heard teachers within these traditions tell their students to let go of attachment and desire. It is a relatively easy concept to think about, but the reality of letting go of both is much harder, especially today. If we try to achieve this – if we try at all – we slip into the desire mode, meaning this wish to do something overcomes our ability to actually do it. So on goes the cycle.

Over the years, I have found that the only way for me to start to achieve this is by developing a practice. I find that by applying concepts and thoughts about these subjects I achieve the opposite of what I am looking for. I prefer doing something and practice can start me on the path to letting go of attachment and desire.

I believe it is vital for us to develop daily practice, even if just for five or ten minutes at first, slowly building up our skill base. I am hoping, over time, you will start to feel the positive effects of your developing practice and naturally want to spend a little more time enjoying these new experiences of sense and feeling.

Finding Time to Develop Your Practice

With this time, I want you to sit quietly and comfortably. Tune into the softness in your breathing, allowing, accepting and observing everything that comes up and bring your attention gently back to your breath.

If you are struggling with any part of this, just accept that you are finding it difficult, then soften your shoulders, your chest, your hips, relaxing your physical body as much as you can and then refocus on your breath.

Once you start to feel your thoughts softening, relaxing and becoming neutral, I want you to ask your body what time would be best to spend ten to fifteen minutes a day on developing your practice. For each of us a different time will suit.

I like to do these techniques twice a day: first thing in the morning, before I get up, and again in the early evening, after I finish work and before dinner. Practising at these times sets me up at the beginning of the day and relaxes me at the end of it.

It is best to play about with this – often it is a matter of being able to find a few quiet minutes, especially difficult if you have young children, when you are either constantly on the go or too exhausted to do anything. If you have young kids, then it's almost more important to find those ten minutes: it will allow you to deal with your day easier and everyone will benefit.

Make an honest pact with yourself to spend at least ten minutes a day developing your practice.

CHAPTER 6

POSTURE

Let's talk for a moment about the importance of posture. I have previously said that we can do this work in any position, as it is mainly perceptual work, but I wish to talk a bit about posture when we are sitting down.

SITTING POSITIONS

Buddhist, Taoist and Hindu traditions tend to employ similar sitting practice positions called full lotus position or pyramid posture. In this posture, as depicted in statues of the Buddha of Compassion, the heels are turned upwards towards the face. This is not easy to do unless you are very flexible or have been in training. A lot of meditational practices talk of sitting through the pain and hours of discomfort sat in this posture, or as close as you can get.

I have done this many times, with varying degrees of success. My legs are much more supple now than when I was a child and teenager, but I still lose feeling in them after being in a classic sitting posture for too long. The benefit of sitting with legs crossed, to some degree, is that it creates a wide base: the idea of a pyramid, with our legs and open hips forming the base and the top of our head being the apex. This gives a good spinal posture.

As an osteopath, I am very aware of the importance of freedom in the spinal joints positively affecting the nerve supply to the internal organs. Each spinal segment has a variety of nerve roots and paths that pass through it. Freedom within each segment seems to enhance the freedom of these nerves and through them to the actual blood supply itself and so to the internal organs. It makes sense that many of the traditions advocate good spinal posture.

The problem with sitting in chairs is that we tend to slump, dropping our spines and compressing the vertebrae. If we sit with our hips apart, it naturally makes the spine straighten. This is a good start. From here, we can start to lengthen the spine.

POSTURES VITAL FOR ENERGY

The Taoists talk of the pyramid posture being vital for energy to start to flow naturally in the energy channels, which they believed were central in the body – the large central meridians. As one would sink into the pyramidal form, it would allow energy to naturally rise and be transformed. Also, when sitting correctly, we tend to be able to breathe more easily and the quality of our breathing is better. If our spines are straight, the the diaphragm can sit freely and move more naturally, allowing the mechanism of breathing to be stronger and freer. This becomes important as our practice develops.

If we allow our sitting bones to really make contact with the surface on which we sit, it helps to give us a sense of grounding, of being connected more strongly to the earth. This is also important.

PRACTISING IN ANY POSITION

In summary, yes, we can practise in any position: my first daily practice is with me lying supine (on my back) in bed. However, if we practise lying down when we are tired, we can fall asleep very quickly – which is OK, but we still need to do our practice!

We can do these techniques standing up on the underground; we can do them while running – which I do often. I practise them while painting, and while I'm treating patients – in fact, in any situation. I also believe it serves to spend ten minutes a day developing a sitting practice.

PRACTICE 6

Sitting Position

Begin the practice

First, find a comfortable room that is quiet and, hopefully, where you won't be disturbed. Bring a glass of water in case you become thirsty. Switch off your phone – just for ten minutes.

Often the best place to practise is on the softness of a sofa, a bed or a comfy chair, but the floor is also perfectly fine. For comfort, I tend to place a pillow under my bottom – this means my legs don't pull when I cross them. Use as many pillows or rolled-up towels as you need to feel comfortable. You may also need to place a rolled-up towel under each knee to support them and reduce the pulling effect that occurs. Above all, make yourself as comfortable as possible.

Notes:

1. The more you are able to practise, the less supports you will need.

2. If you have hip restrictions, or problems with your knees or back, sit up straight on a good chair with your feet firmly on the floor.

3. You do not need to sit in the full-or half-lotus position unless you are able to do so easily.

Straighten the spine

Now that you're sitting down comfortably, begin to straighten the spine and bring a degree of balance to your body. First, soften your breathing and relax your body. Is there anywhere in your body that feels tight or uncomfortable? If so, move a little and try to direct your outbreath towards the area. As you breathe out, relax that part and try to feel as if you are breathing out the tightness.

As you begin to become more comfortable and relaxed, try to feel the area where your head meets your neck at the back. This, in most of us, is locked – the head tends to sit back on the neck and lock it down. Envision this space between the head and neck, and gently nod your head downwards. As you look down towards the floor, it opens the space between your head and neck. When you start to sit, you need to open this space and you may look downwards. Ideally, you want to gaze at a point a couple of metres in front of you and sustain it.

Sense the space between head and neck

Once you open this space, you tend to find the rest of your neck lengthens a bit to compensate. Allow your neck to lengthen. It may help to visualize a string attached to the crown of your head exerting a gentle pull upwards, very slowly.

Feel the lengthening of the spine

You will hopefully start to feel the spine lengthening from the top down. Enjoy the sense of space coming and, for any stuck sections, breathe out the tension and always try to soften and lengthen at the same time.

Feel the spine lengthening between your shoulders. As it lengthens, allow your shoulders to widen, as if they could hang freely. Allow your chest to relax and sink just a little. Now soften it and breathe out any tensions.

Feel your lower back lengthening

Let your stomach soften and your breathing relax. You will start to feel your lower back lengthening from the top down and your pelvis beginning to relax. As you do this, you should find that your hips naturally want to widen. As your hips widen, let your legs soften and relax, all the way down to your feet and toes.

Conclusion

What you are doing here is relaxing but lengthening and straightening your spine so that your organs can enjoy a free nerve and blood supply. This, too, will help you as you deepen your practice.

Just enjoy sitting here in comfort, observing the softness in your breath, accepting, allowing and observing anything that comes up in your mind in terms of thoughts, feelings and sensations. You should experience a sense here of understanding that each thought or feeling or sensation is connected to either an attachment from the past or a desire for the future. Never judge these sensations, simply watch them pass across your blue sky or your blank canvas.

Try to enjoy just sitting. After a while, a sensation of discomfort will arise – it always does. Observe this for a few moments, then stop there, don't fight through it. Your tolerance time will improve by the day.

CHAPTER 7

THE STILLNESS
BEHIND EVERYTHING

We live in a world full of noise, where it is hard to find real silence. Even in wild places there are birds singing and the noise of the wind. Occasionally, if we wake up in the hour before dawn, in the quiet of the night, we can experience a real stillness. This stillness has a particular, amazing quality – a huge dynamic energy, an aliveness, a power. We can sense the stillness with our whole body, can almost hear it, like a hum, but more so. It has a quality that we feel.

SILENT STILLNESS

Mountaineers sometimes report having experienced a similar sensation way up high in the snow, when the winds drop and they become enveloped by an enormous, silent stillness. The mountaineers describe this as powerful, almost overwhelming, like sensing the throb of the universe. Hindu and Buddhist religions talk of the ohm sound, the sound of the universe humming or the underlying love that connects all.

Is it possible to sense this quality in our everyday lives? Can you imagine how we could feel if our senses were connected in this way at all times? To sense this stillness, we must first quieten our internal noise, the sound of the relentless actions and reactions of our minds.

As we start to find a quiet neutral in ourselves, an amazing thing begins to happen. Our senses that have been bombarded and in a constant state of being overwhelmed can start to quieten, to soften and open, as if they can really start to breathe. As this happens, we begin to really hear that bird singing and sometimes to almost sense why it is singing. As this neutral develops in us, and as we practise, it becomes easier to sense a great stillness that is always there, behind the sounds. We can start to feel it in our body, and even hear it.

It's an odd concept really. How can we hear stillness? I think tuning in to stillness engages a different part of our sense of hearing, which is almost on a different vibration: a kind of felt-sense that we feel and hear together. It is difficult to explain but easier to sense.

We all use our senses slightly differently when we try to become aware of things that exist on the edge of our perception, such as sensing stillness. For me, it helps to try to hear a certain quality of sound. I can, at first, access this with my hearing. From there, it's possible to go on to sense it with my whole body.

A QUIET, POWERFUL HUM

To try to get a sense of stillness, I first let myself be present to all the sounds around me, then try to hear or feel something quiet behind those sounds. The sound, for me, is not quite a hiss but between a hiss and a throb – maybe a quiet hum – but the feeling you get when you hear it is one of power. Maybe this is best described as a quiet, powerful hum. When you start to hear and feel it, you will have your own way of describing it. Also, its quality varies, albeit slightly. I wonder if that is because the sound or feeling changes, or, more likely, our senses vary a little in their function.

As we develop our practice, I am interested in engaging and developing our ability to shift our perception so that eventually it is free to be moved by the moment and the great tides, the rhythms within nature, and stillness around us. Here, we are not looking for internal stillness, but learning to perceive a stillness that is always there, around and outside us, but also in us.

The best thing about this work is that it just feels great. As we connect more to stillness and learn to access it directly at any moment, our body and mind want more connections.

The Stillness Behind Everything

Begin the practice

As you sit, spend a few minutes turning your awareness to the quietness, softness and delicacy in your breathing. Let all thoughts come and then let them go, passing like clouds, all the while allowing your attention to naturally return to the softness in your breathing. If you slightly lengthen your outbreath so it is longer than your inbreath, this will calm your system quicker.

Breathe out tension

With each outbreath, allow yourself to relax your body more, focus on breathing in sweet softness and breathing out tensions. As your sense of neutral comes, your body starts to relax. It is almost as if the tight grip your mind has on your body starts to relax and soften, and your senses begin to open. Let your thoughts and sensations come and go, not focusing too deeply on them. Just watch them come and go. Try not to focus even on the developing sense of quiet in you. Fully allow everything and let your mind breathe.

Bring attention to your hearing

Let yourself be aware of all the sounds, from the plumbing, to the birds, to your tummy rumbling. Let these sounds arise and then sense the quiet between them. It is almost as if the sounds arise and fall away within the quiet.

Sense with your whole body

Now listen to the quiet behind the sounds. Start to get a sense of that great stillness that lies behind everything. It has a tonal quality that you can feel as much as hear. It is deeply calming, yet so very alive.

Conclusion

In the beginning, you can only get a few seconds of sensing this stilless. If you sit with it and your bodies learn to recognize and respond to it, this great stillness remains with you for longer periods. It can sometimes start to give you the sensation that you are being held by life and all is well, a sense of resting in the great natural peace.

$\mathscr{P}$URE $\mathscr{A}$TTENTION

How often do we give something our full attention? If we are eating, we are also talking and checking our texts; if we are watching TV, we are talking and eating; if we are walking the dog, we are on the phone or thinking about something we must do tomorrow. When are we really present to the activity we are undertaking?

As a child, I remember watching a craftsperson at work or someone doing something they were skilled at and loved. As they focused their attention completely and abandoned themselves to the task at hand, it seemed that they generated a gentle, sweet energy – it was literally palpable. I wanted to be around them as they worked, and I didn't want to leave. I remember sensing that energy as a young child and I am still drawn to it today.

TOTAL ATTENTION AND PURE AWARENESS

That sweet, soft energy seems to be generated by total attention and pure awareness without a splitting or scattering of intent – pure energy focused on the task at hand. It is wonderful to experience. The energy feels a bit like love – and what could feel better?

The opposite, of course, can also be true. If we are emotional, be it happy or sad, if our nervous systems are on full alert and we are distressed about something, then the energy around us is disturbed. It is easy to sense this energy. When we are in these alert states, it doesn't matter how beautiful the sunset is in front of us, we don't fully see it. We may glance up and register it, but we do not really feel and take in its beauty – it seems impossible at that moment for us to be moved by it.

Why do people say that something moves them? Maybe, it is like there is a connection to a deep part of us that is engaged by that sunset, or a story, and there is a moment of grace. What if we could train our brains to have less noise in among the stress and distress, so that we can be still enough to 'smell the roses' more of the time? How much more beautiful could life be?

BEING DISCONNECTED

How often do we approach anything in life with pure attention? How often do we meet an object or a person without any preconceived ideas about them? How often do we really look at a tree or object without naming, quantifying or judging it? How much of our lives is spent reacting to our ideas and thoughts about a person or a loved one, without really seeing them in the moment? When we do this, we are relating to concepts and not real things. This is harmful to us as it disconnects us from one another and from nature.

It is so hard not to react to patterns of behaviour in friends and family, but the more we are aware of our reactions, the less we enter conflict. Becoming aware of our reactions is the basis of psychotherapy and cognitive behavioural therapies, but it only goes halfway. We need to step beyond this and let go of all concepts of another person so that we can meet them totally free of any history of reactions or views. This seems an almost impossible task, but if we can go a little bit in that direction, it will open up a great deal of beauty to us – in relationships with one another and, again, in nature.

OUR FULL ATTENTION

When we give our full attention to whatever we are doing, something amazing happens. The activity brings a sense of stillness within its motion and generates a beautiful energy. This is something that other people want to be around. It brings us into a state of pure awareness, without our energy being in too many places at once.

Because each thought, emotion and feeling has energy, our thoughts and emotions can be scattered in too many directions, our energy dissipated. This dispersal of energy is exhausting. If our energy is pure and focused, we become better at whatever activity we are doing, which, in turn, makes that activity more enjoyable.

Wild animals give whatever they are doing their focused attention. A cheetah in full flight, hunting, is the epitome of stillness in action; it may be running at sixty miles an hour but, with full awareness and attention on its prey, there is a quiet stillness within its extreme activity.

When teaching osteopaths to understand anatomy, I try to help them open their senses and feel subtle processes within the body. I start by trying to de-educate them. We learn anatomy by looking at books and dissections. When doing so, we are learning from something that is two-dimensional and certainly not living, breathing tissue, which looks and feels totally different. The danger for students is that they can apply concepts to what they are trying to feel and, in doing so, could limit their perception and their ability to feel processes in living tissue.

A NEW LEVEL OF AWARENESS

When studying, I encourage them to try to let go of concepts and pictures and attempt to really feel. It's hard to do so at the beginning, but if I encourage my students to be creative and think of colour, shape and emotion, they often start to get a sense of the living tissue below their hands. Over time, the students start to feel the living anatomy and perceptual clarity can begin to develop.

For this exercise, let us try to let go of any concepts. This is hard to do, but if we can achieve it just a little, it can open us up to a new level of awareness and perception. Let's also work with being present enough to give whatever we are doing our full attention.

PRACTICE 8

Achieving Pure Attention

Beginning the practice

For this practice, you can be anywhere – inside or outside. It is easier, in the beginning, to go outside – for example, looking at a tree or a flower, ideally something not moving too much at first – or you can practise by looking at any object indoors. Try this exercise in a few different locations to see what works for you.

Don't put pressure on yourself to perform this practice perfectly. What you are looking for is a softening of your conceptual grip on judging what you see, which gives space for a purer awareness.

Settle your nervous system

Sit quietly (*see page 37*) and identify an object to focus your attention on. Let your nervous system settle by allowing all thoughts, but by bringing your awareness to something quiet or soft in your breathing. To do this, breathe softer and sense this softness in your breath.

Feel the underlying stillness

When you start to settle, allow your senses to feel the stillness behind everything. This sense is almost audible – it feels as if it is on the edge of your hearing. Once you get a sense of this stillness, it will become easier to tune into each time you practise.

From here, allow your awareness to rest on the chosen object. Try to let go of any judgements or concepts about the object. Let go of any knowledge you have acquired about it and even any words that could have formed a screen between you and the object you are looking at. Try to really see it as if you are seeing it for the first time. Aim to see the object with all your energy, your whole being and awareness. If you can do this, you may start to notice a sense of clear awareness. This brings a certain stillness and energy to it, just pure, clear attention.

Maintain your awareness

It is hard to maintain this awareness for a long period of time. At the beginning, just for a few seconds, your mind really wants to wander and attach itself to many things. If this happens, just allow it and don't judge it. This is normal. Bring your awareness back to the flower or whatever object you are looking at.

Conclusion

This awareness can engender a sense of awe and even of love. Aim to spend a couple of minutes on this exercise each day, then try to bring the concept into other areas. For example, a great practice is to really listen, with an open mind and an open heart, to whomever you are talking to; just listen, without preparing your thoughts for the next thing you will say. How often do you really hear what another person is saying – letting go of concepts or analysis? How often do you just sit in quiet stillness and listen? Amazingly, this open-hearted listening becomes a blessing – not just for you but also for the person talking to you. It is a wonderful thing to be truly heard.

You can also do this with your other senses. If you really feel whatever you are touching, the experience can be like an act of love. Touch lovingly – even if it is your mobile phone. The interesting thing is that when you apply pure attention, your touch softens a little and slows down naturally.

If you widen your focus and try this in other areas, only focusing on the task at hand – for example, cooking supper with pure attention – what happens? Does the food taste better?

It is also nice to bathe with pure attention: to feel the water cleansing your body and to become aware of the sensations of the water on your skin.

Another way to expand this practice is by walking or running with pure awareness. Your steps get lighter and softer and you connect more to the earth below you. A powerful technique is to walk *love* into the earth, meaning that each step taken implants a feeling of love into the earth. The earth loves this, and so will you. It is amazing to run with pure attention. The running, although you are in movement, has a quality of stillness, like a cheetah running.

You can practise pure attention doing absolutely anything. Life can become a practice, meaning you start to be in a constant process of internal cultivation. The more you do this practice, the more you will feel the benefits. Remember to practise it a few times a day until the process develops into a habit and becomes integrated into your reality.

$\mathcal{F}$INDING $\mathcal{G}$ROUND

We tend to live our lives in our heads, thinking and doing things at every waking moment. The practices we are learning here aim to turn us away from that, to show us how to tune in to our senses and then master our attention so we can focus it where we wish, to develop our relationship with the stillness both in and around us, to become comfortable to live in the moment and to reconnect deeply with nature and its natural tides and flow.

A SENSE OF UNGROUNDEDNESS

If we think of the body as an energy field, and that we are thinking and processing information all day, it follows that the majority of energy must be found in the brain. Indeed, the brain does use up most of the energy produced by the body from the food we consume – there is a lot going on in our brains all the time, which tends to send all our energy upwards and can leave us feeling ungrounded – literally, as if disconnected from the earth we live on. The disconnection worsens when we are not near nature but live and work in buildings far above the ground. This loss of connection, energetically, to the earth can make us feel ungrounded, almost dizzy at times.

While writing, I am thinking and typing and my attention is entirely on what I am trying to say. But, fortunately, I am in a study that looks onto a garden, which today is snowy and sunny. I stop every few minutes, feel the ground beneath my feet and look at the beautiful garden. It helps me stay on subject.

CONNECTING WITH NATURE

I remember as a student in London, I would spend all my spare time in parks with trees – I literally became a tree hugger. On the weekends I would go to Richmond Park, the closest thing to a natural, wild space that I could find, and sit by and tune in to the wonderful trees there. I would find it restorative, so much so that I could engage with the city again.

Trees are very grounding. On my courses, I sometimes get the students to draw a tree. Mostly, they draw the tree they picture in their imagination. Very rarely do they draw the root system, which actually is about half the tree, but unseen. As we know, trees have extensive root systems that penetrate the earth from where they take in the water and minerals they need to grow and survive. We could argue that the roots are the most important part of the tree, essential for its survival. If we think of the great oak trees with their extensive root systems, we begin to get a picture of what it means to be grounded, to be rooted to the ground. This is an important aspect of meditation and sensory development work.

To be rooted, or grounded, also means to be connected. In the same way as an electric circuit needs a wire called 'earth' to protect it, we too need grounding, the sense of rootedness to this earth we live on and love. If we are not 'earthed', we can fly away, into our heads, and consequently, we can become disconnected and even anxious. But how do we reconnect to this earth, to this rooted, grounded way of being? Do we need to have our 'feet on the ground' to be grounded?

If you think of a woodsman in the forest, or a gardener or farmer, if you watch them at work, they tend everything in a gentle, slow and methodical manner – there is no great rush or agitation. It is quite the opposite to the fast, stressed, high-octane pace of workers on

Wall Street or in the City of London. Which would we consider more grounded? For me, the folks working with nature seem naturally grounded. I think it comes from working within the natural world; they quietly fall into its rhythms without even considering it. But we cannot all give up our jobs and work with nature. We need to bring nature with us as we are nature, we are a part of nature and the more we reconnect with it, the more naturally grounded we are.

FEELING GROUNDED

Until we have been practising these techniques for a while, we need to learn a few tricks. Can we feel grounded while in the crazy city, surrounded by sensory overload and fast living?

· First, recall what we talked about in Chapter 3 on timing and tempo (*see pages 22–3*). If we just slow down a tiny bit – walk slower, think slower and relax a little – our energy feels like it drops back into our body.

· Other ways to ground yourself include finding time to be in nature, such as tending the garden, which is a wonderful way.

· We can also start to ground ourselves by focusing our energy away from our head, such as with a foot massage.

· Dancing is another excellent way to reconnect with the earth. By moving on the dance floor, we become grounded and relaxed – while also having fun.

· Standing practices, such the yoga warrior poses, naturally connect us with the earth as gravity is on our side.

Now let's explore a few grounding practices.

Grounding

Beginning the practice

The perfect place to practise this is, of course, in a quiet garden, standing in close proximity to a tree. But, actually, you can do this anywhere, any time.

You can do this practice sitting, but I think it is easier in a standing posture. Stand comfortably with your feet shoulder-width apart. Drop your knees a little so they are in line with your toes. If that is uncomfortable, don't worry, stand straight or sit down. Allow your arms to hang, relaxed by your sides. Let your chest drop a little and relax.

Bring attention to your feet

Draw your attention to the bottom of your mid-foot. Can you feel the sock you are wearing? (Ideally, this practice is done outside in a warm spot with no socks or shoes on, but you can do it just as easily with them on.) Once you are aware of the feeling of the sock, allow your attention to expand to also feel your shoes. This sense of proprioception (the neurological ability of the body to sense movement and position) is totally normal – you use it all the time without even considering it.

Expand your attention

Feel the ground you are standing on. Is it a soft carpet, a wooden floor, concrete or wet grass? Can you feel it? Expand your attention a little further; send it about 15 centimetres (6 inches) into the ground beneath you and immediately you will feel a connection. It almost feels as if your centre of gravity strengthens; it feels good. It's as if the earth comes up to meet you. This is harder to do if you are not at ground level, but it is possible if you are higher up – you just have to send your attention deeper until it hits the ground.

Be careful if you feel at all dizzy; 'grounding' can cause your blood pressure to drop a little, so go gently if you are prone to low blood pressure. Conversely, do this exercise a lot if you are prone to high blood pressure – it is good for you.

Connect to the earth

Relax into the feeling of being connected to the earth around you. It feels like a wonderful and totally natural way to be. If you spend a few minutes sensing the earth, you can then expand your attention all around you

to the earth as a whole, and feel yourself connected to the entire planet. This sense of connection can be difficult to achieve at first, but sometimes the sense of the earth as a whole will come to you naturally.

Conclusion

Whenever you are feeling agitated, ungrounded or irritable, try this practice for a couple of minutes and you will find it calming, grounding and relaxing.

CHAPTER 10

THE FLOW

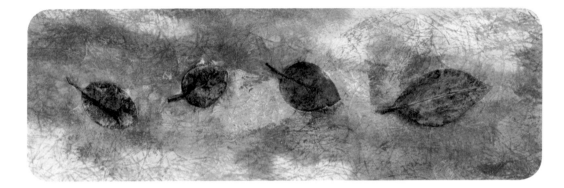

Lao Tzu (or Laozi) was a mysterious figure, whose name literally means 'old master'. He is reputed to be the author of the Chinese classic text *Tao Te Ching* and the founder of Taoism (pronounced Daoism). He is a mysterious figure partly because it has been debated in some academic circles whether he even existed, though it is widely believed that he lived in China in the sixth century BCE.

It is said that, at eighty years of age, Lao Tzu grew tired of the excesses of normal life. He went to live as a hermit at the western gate of the city of Chengzhou. The sentry on the gate listened to his wise words and encouraged him to write a book. This is reputedly the story of the birth of the famous work called the *Tao Te Ching*. The guard was so impressed with the old man's view of the world that he left his post and became his first disciple. Other stories about Lao Tzu include one that he travelled to India and became a teacher to Siddhartha Gautama, the Buddha.

THE SOURCE OF EVERYTHING

The Tao, according to Taoism, is the source of everything. It describes the unmanifest nature from which everything arises. Taoism calls for its students to return to a natural state, in harmony with the Tao – to be in the natural flow of life.

The concept of Wu Wei lies at the heart of the teachings. Wu Wei is non-action, or not forcing, or flowing with the moment. This implies that to be with the Tao – the very nature of things – we need to be in a state of flow, like swimming in a flowing river. We either relax and flow downstream or we try to head upstream – against the flow – which is exhausting.

GOING WITH THE FLOW

Going with the flow seems to be the simplest advice in the world, but how often do we do it? More often, we are disconnected from knowing where the flow is. We tend to apply concepts and thinking and drive ourselves on in our lives without even sensing the natural flow of things and without even knowing how to feel the flow. This makes life difficult for us.

If we could start to become aware of the metaphorical river we are in, then we could become aware of the flow. We could try to go with the flow and life could become easier and less tiring. But how on earth do we go about finding the flow of things? Maybe, to start with, we can try to let go of any concept of destination. If we step off the bank in a metaphorical river, we enter the natural flow of it. We cannot decide to flow upriver if the flow is down; we must just step in and go with it.

Our problem is that mostly we want to go the opposite way. Governed by our wishes, desires and emotions, certain actions and thinking can lead us against, and have us fighting with, the natural flow of things. When we go against the flow, it can be exhausting.

We must let go of this idea of going against the flow. To try to do that, what if we just take that first step into the flow of the river and see where it takes us? It would certainly be less tiring.

Sometimes life grabs us and takes us in a direction that is beyond our control. It is like we are stepping into a very fast-flowing river. In this instance, we have no option but to go with the current or we will drown.

The difficulty of allowing ourselves to go with the flow arises when the flow is gentle, in these times it is hard to sense the natural flow of things and to know which way the flow is going. Sometimes, the object or goal is visible just a bit upstream and we try to swim against the current to reach it. But this tires us and we get nowhere. We all know that feeling. But if we just hop in and relax, there may be a far greater goal around the next bend that was just beyond our vision from the bank.

It seems that, to be in the flow of things or in the Tao which, according to Taoism, is the source of everything, we first need a quiet mind. If there is too much noise, how can we sense anything? Going with the flow also suggests that we can see beyond ourselves sense the bigger flow in the things around us, like stepping into a river and seeing beyond the bank to where the river is flowing. This implies that we are paying attention to what is around us.

SIGNS IN NATURE

Many indigenous tribes of the world paid attention to signs in nature and learnt to read them. The Bushmen of the Kalahari, the Australian Aborigines and the Native Americans could all see and track signs in nature for many purposes. They could use signs in nature to read weather patterns, to track animals and to follow songlines (ancestral pathways).

In our modern, Western lives, we have lost a great deal of that contact with nature. Our lives are more complex and there is an overstimulation of the senses. With this complexity, how can we read the subtle signs around us? And there are always signs around us, whether it is the subtle shift in mood of a friend, a certain action that we are trying to carry out that is proving tricky, or the change in air pressure preceding a storm. All these signs can tell us something if we take the time and effort to stop and look, like standing on the bank and seeing the way the river is flowing. These signs make us look beyond our thoughts, feelings and emotions and allow us to sense a bigger picture.

Why then, instead of thinking things out, don't we try to feel things out a bit? Next time you are unsure about a decision, ask yourself, 'Am I going with the flow here?' Or, 'What is the flow here?'

We have lost that direct rapport with nature and our own perception of what is obvious to do. Instead, we have learnt to apply logic. This works, up to a point, but it does not stop us from swimming upstream for most of our lives. And, as we have said before, this is exhausting and stressful.

Going with the flow doesn't mean avoiding responsibilities and not facing up to reality. Lao Tzu spent time talking about social duty and leadership, about taking responsibility for community and for country. The early Taoists would not spend much of their time in temples, preferring to be immersed in culture and society. From the midst of community, they taught about entering a place of stillness from which choice could be clearly made.

FACING OUR FEARS

To go with this deeper flow in life, this underlying nature of things, we need greater self-awareness. To develop this greater self-awareness, we need the courage to face our fears and to let ourselves be free to be moved by the tide of life. To reconnect with the natural great flow of life, we need three things:

1. To find a sense of quiet in our minds, a degree of neutral – a quiet stillness.

2. To reconnect with nature and the natural tides in nature, which we will start to do in the next chapter (*see pages 57–9*).

3. To face our fears and emotions through the practice of acceptance, allowing and observing, which we began trying in Chapter 2 (*see pages 16–20*).

We will return to Taoist practices of meditation, and internal alchemy, one of the roots of this practice, later in Chapter 17 (*see pages 87–91*).

Going with the Flow

Begin the practice

First, apply what you already know about quietening your mind:

A sense of being in your body

You need awareness, a sense of being in your body, which you can do by tuning in to your breathing, but with no judgement. You can also do this by feeling something delicate and soft in your breath, with any part or all of the body. What you are doing is bringing your awareness, and energy, back into your body.

Accepting, allowing and observing

Next, practice accepting, allowing and observing. It doesn't matter if you are stressed, or if you are in pain or not, allow and accept whatever state you are in.

Develop a sense of your surroundings

Things are now becoming quiet, fluid and open. Get a sense of your surroundings. You live in a fluid world. Try to feel this sense of fluidity as you did in the previous practice. What does fluid feel like? Maybe a trickling soft warmth, or a sense of a babbling stream, gently flowing, or just the feeling of a liquid.

Be receptive to a sense of fluidity

Open your awareness to the space around you, either in the room you are currently in or in the surrounding natural world. Use your feeling sense to try and notice a soft fluidity. Open your awareness to your surroundings and be receptive to a sense of fluidity in things.

As you sit quietly open your awareness to potential movements within this fluid world, which is all around you with its natural ebbs and flows. Let this fluidity hold your body and support it. Let the air around you act like a fluid. Wait there until this fluidity moves you into action.

Here, you have started to explore the idea that you live in a potentially fluid world. If you step into your metaphorical river, the current can take you. This requires trusting something outside yourself and outside of your thinking world. Do this gradually. It is a big step if you are unused to trusting life and it can bring up emotions. If it does, apply the three tenets of acceptance: that you can have the emotion, allow the emotion and start to observe it, but not be owned by it.

CHAPTER 11

OUR FLUID BODY

'Nothing in the world is as soft and yielding as water.
Yet for dissolving the hard and inflexible, nothing
can surpass it. The soft overcomes the hard; the gentle
overcomes the rigid. Everyone knows this is true,
but few can put it into practice.'

Lao Tzu, *Tao Te Ching*

Our bodies are ninety per cent fluid, of which seventy per cent is water. Some of the latest research in the development of embryos suggests that we could develop and form as groups of fluid fields, or different fluid masses. These fields of fluid slowly move and interact with one another. This has the effect of changing the fields and even the cells, which go on to start to form tissue. The groups of forming cells then come together, creating structures and starting to function as vessels, organs, the brain and so on.

In my work as an osteopath, we learn to feel and sense function in the body, from joint movements to more subtle fluid motion. We try to feel the gentle expression and breathing of fluid fields in the body. As a person's body relaxes, they seem to become more fluid.

Our language reflects this idea of fluidity. We talk of people relaxing and becoming more fluid, taking on less fixed and more fluid viewpoints. Here, fluidity implies more freedom, a softening.

When we strain a muscle or a joint, the process of inflammation and repair has an effect of creating hard, fibrous, solid tissue within the damaged tissues. This is not a permanent thing; it is part of the healing process. At a later stage, this hardness begins to soften again. The fibrous tissue is reabsorbed by the body and things start to become fluid-like again as healing nears completion.

The problem often comes when the localized tissue damage remains and cannot go through the final stage of softening back to normal. That is when things can get stuck and symptoms continue for longer than they should. As osteopaths, we find these areas of hard tissue and, using gentle manipulation techniques, act to restore a degree of fluidity to the local tissues.

FLUIDITY AND SOFTNESS

Taoist philosophy talks about fluidity and softness, the softness and yielding water over-coming even the solidity of rock.

When our lives undergo a big change – the end of a relationship or the loss of a loved one – if we remain fixed in our old ways of thinking, the pain can go on for longer than it should. But if we remain fluid in our thinking, there is a good chance that we will be able to adapt to the new circumstance quicker and more easily.

Have you seen footage of a cheetah running? It is fluid and effortless. Our perception of our own body, however, is not that of fluidity but of rigid bone structures holding us up. We are highly aware of areas of our body when they are blocked or in pain. These areas do not feel at all fluid, in fact. If we could sense a degree of fluidity within our body, it could help us to relax and change our awareness from what feels blocked to what feels fluid and healthy.

If we start to soften in our perception of ourselves and others, it seems to have the effect of letting things breathe a little. But if we don't learn to yield, we may become fixed in a position, which may have a blocking effect on us.

STRENGTH IN FLUIDITY

Fluidity can also mean strength, just as the fluid movement of water will eventually wear away rock. If we can build a deepening relationship with our internal fluidity, it can lead to a general softening in our self-perception. It can encourage us to get in touch with our internal self-correcting processes, which keep us healthy and balanced. As with everything we have done so far, we are in a process of developing our sensory awareness and that needs practise. The results will come with time and steady work, so here we will try to sense and feel our fluid body.

Sensing Your Fluid Body

Begin the practice

Start by spending a few minutes getting a sense of the softness in your breathing. Remember to fully allow whatever thoughts or feelings arise and gently bring back your awareness to the delicacy, softness and even fluidity in your breath.

Once you relax and feel neutral, open your awareness to your whole body. Feel areas that are tight and stiff. Let your awareness of these areas be light and fluid; let it move freely, don't focus on one point or problem.

Change your focus

Try to get a sense of something in your body that feels fluid. If this is hard, try to sense a part of you that feels OK, happy, light. If you are in pain, try to focus on the part of you that is not.

When you start to feel this tiny fluid movement, it is fleeting – a microsecond of something that disappears and then can reappear somewhere else. This is what you are looking for, what you would call 'potency' in the body. If you look too closely, it disappears, so maintain a very light, almost soft focus. If your perception becomes too focused and rigid and you employ thinking too much, you will lose it. This is purely a perceptual, feeling thing. If you cannot feel this, then bring your awareness back to the softness in your breath and stay with that for a few moments, then try again.

Feel the fluidity

At the beginning, you will only be able to feel this fluidity for short periods. As your practice deepens, you will start to feel this beautiful fluidity in more and more of your own body.

As you develop your practice, you will go on to feel your body as one drop of fluid. The fluidity that you detect in parts will eventually become a whole fluid body acting as one, which brings a sense of wholeness, harmony and even peacefulness. This perceptual skill takes time to develop and you must go through stages in your perception and feeling. The important thing here is to practise the steps and allow, accept and observe any difficulties you are having. Don't get bogged down and don't think – this is purely a feeling process.

SECTION

II

PLACE
and BEING

CHAPTER 12

THE STORY ON THE WIND

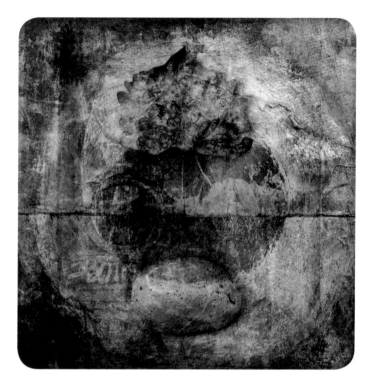

The word 'psyche' comes from the Greek for breath or gust of wind. The word spirit comes from the Latin *spiritus*, which again signifies both breath and wind. Until the time of Socrates and Plato, the wind and air were seen by all cultures as sacred elements connecting all of us, including nature with its mountains, seas, animals and plants. The Greek philosophers sought to change the emphasis to a more person-centred world view. Judeo-Christian philosophy focused on God being outside and above us, creating but not necessarily within nature.

62

THE BUSHMEN OF THE KALAHARI

The indigenous tribes sensed that awareness was not incorporated within a person; rather, it was carried on the wind and connected us all. Socratic thinking brought this sense of awareness and the idea of the psyche inside the realm of the body. Christianity has firmly sought to externalize God as a power that is not within and around us and in nature, but otherworldly and separate.

The Navajo believe that wind is present in a person from the moment of conception, when two winds, one from each parent, form a single wind within the embryo. They say it is the motion of the wind within the growing embryo or foetus that produces growth and development. The Navajo believe that when an infant is born this internal wind links with an external wind, which surrounds and enters the baby. The wind that surrounds the Navajo, they believe, grants life, movement, speech and awareness, and connects all beings. It is thought to act as the means of communication between all things in the animate world.

Laurens van der Post did a lot to document the ways of the Bushmen of the Kalahari. The explorer was brought up at the turn of the twentieth century on a large farm on the borders of the Kalahari Desert in Africa. He spent many years, since his earliest memories, in the company of the Bushmen, hunting and farming. They were quite unlike other African peoples, being small in stature, lighter skinned and with almost Aboriginal features. The Bushmen lived a life always on the move and were amazing hunters.

Van der Post has written many books about the Bushmen, including *The Lost World of the Kalahari* (1958) and *The Heart of the Hunter* (1961), documenting the amazing ways of this timeless African tribe. These tribes became persecuted by newer tribes in Africa and their freedom to hunt and live a nomadic life was curtailed by land ownership.

TRIBAL SENSORY PERCEPTION OF NATURE

In his books, Van der Post tells stories about the Bushmen's incredible sensory perception of nature. They could detect a wild animal many miles away on the plains, and talked about the stories coming to them on the wind. This amazing perceptual awareness would bring with it a deep instinctual knowledge of the nature around them. This knowledge enabled the Bushmen to live for months in the Kalahari Desert, hunting wild animals and finding water.

In stark contrast to this heightened awareness, when Van der Post entered a town with the Bushmen he observed that they lost all their instincts and would be very uncomfortable and irritable. The Bushmen would say that they had lost connection with the wind and would need to drink alcohol to cope. But when the Bushmen left the town, they would soften, calm and be visibly restored as soon as they felt the wind. What was it about wind that connected the Bushmen of the Kalahari to nature and themselves, and brought them immediate peace and calm?

This story is repeated in other aboriginal peoples. I lived for six months with the Mayans in Guatemala, treating them and learning their ways. They talked of a loss of connection to the nature around them, through exploitation and political upheaval, which caused distrust and disharmony within tribes and even families. I treated people still shocked and traumatized from the Civil War, displaying a wide variety of symptoms.

THE 'GREAT' OR 'LONG' TIDE

William Sutherland, one of the earliest osteopaths practising at the beginning of the twentieth century, would work on patients with gentle hands-on techniques. Sometimes, he noticed at certain times in the treatments, the room would quieten. A deep sense of stillness would be present and from the stillness this gentle, quiet, fluid tide – not water, but fluid in its feeling – would enter the room. This sensation would infuse the patient, the practitioner and the room, and the treatment process seemed to improve. This slow, fluid motion has been termed the 'great or long tide' by osteopaths Rollin Becker and James Jealous – 'the wind' to the Bushmen of the Kalahari – and its movement is so natural and peaceful that both practitioner and patient would be able to feel it.

It is possible for anyone to sense this delicate fluidity on the edge of our perception and it is wonderful when we feel this great tide that seems to connect us all. This feeling is very healing and calming in quality and it feels as though we are deeply connected with nature.

When teaching students on the course to feel this great tide, everyone could feel it, but there seem to be certain prerequisites. First, we need to be in a place of quiet neutral, where our nervous systems are not in overdrive and we are calm. Next, we need to try to open our awareness to the stillness behind everything, as we did in the previous chapters. From here if we wait with our attention way out on the horizon, as we will learn in the practice that follows this chapter, we will start to feel this great fluid tide in motion.

The tide feels like the most natural thing in the world and it is amazing to sense it. It seems that we start to feel almost breathed by nature, as if we are part of this tide ourselves, which acts to deeply connect us with nature. We can relax and literally go with the flow. Going with the flow is, in my opinion, borne from being connected to the tide. It is a state where we are not being driven by the workings of our psyche, but by a slower, natural and more instinctual force. This could be what Taoists call 'being with the Tao'. We will develop our thinking on the great tide in the next chapter.

In my view, what we call the tide is like the wind of the Bushmen of the Kalahari and the Navajo. It seems like a wind that can connect and inform us, seeming to deepen our connection to our health and nature around us. It can potentially connect us with more instinctual elements within ourselves, bringing qualities of peace and calmness.

The Bigger Breath
(The Story on the Wind)

Begin the practice

Sit comfortably and start to do the usual steps to bring a degree of neutrality to your nervous system. Practise accepting, allowing and then observing your thoughts, feelings and emotions. Bring your awareness to your breathing and do not judge it, just watch the breath as it enters and leaves your body.

Broaden awareness of the breath

After a few minutes you may start to feel a certain softness and warmth in your chest. Allow that feeling and just broaden your awareness to the movement of the breath. As you breathe in and out, really sense the feeling of the air as it hits your nostrils and your trachea and your lungs – this is an amazing feeling, isn't it? You are sensing something that cannot be seen, yet breath gives you life and is connected to everything else on this earth.

The Native American Lakota tribes would smoke the pipe to see the movements of smoke in the air and to sense the connection between each person and the surrounding air. You do not need to smoke to sense this connection. There is a unification between yourself and everything and you are sensing that in your body.

Sense the weight of air on your skin

Bring your attention to your skin and see if you can sense the weight of the air on it. It's a subtle feeling, but once you tune in, you can feel it.

Open your feeling sense

You are surrounded by this air and breathe it. It connects you and holds you. Try to sense a degree of stillness in the air around and within you. Open your awareness wider and try to sense this connecting air around you as far as to the horizon. Let your feeling sense – a sensing, a feeling, of the space around you – open, as if all your senses are breathing out.

Conclusion

As you deepen and broaden your sensory awareness, start to deepen your connection with the ever-present stillness in and around you.

CHAPTER 13

THE GREAT TIDE

At the University of Pennsylvania in the 1950s, a botanist called William Seifriz recorded a wonderful video of a slime mould. Slime mould is an undifferentiated fluid mass of protoplasm without cell membranes. The video shows a slow, rhythmic motion of the mould breathing in and out in cycles of around fifty seconds. This breathing movement is clearly visible.

This slow and gentle rhythm is one we can find elsewhere in nature and even within our bodies. We could perceive it as a slow, fluid flow that originates from stillness, which moves and *breathes* living forms. This slow, cyclic rising and ebbing is like a slow tide, not normally visible except in the mould, but it is possible to learn to feel this in living things and between living things, like a slow, fluid motion.

It seems easier to perceive this tidal movement when we are in nature, sitting quietly, and when we are aware of a certain stillness in and around us. From that place, it is possible sometimes to perceive, just on the edge of our senses, this fluid, wind-like quality arising from the stillness at the horizon and moving slowly towards us. This is the great tide.

This great tide has been documented in many cultures. The Tibetan Buddhists call it the 'unconditioned winds of the vital forces'. The Navajo have named it the 'nilch'i' or 'holy wind'. The Bushmen of the Kalahari refer to it as the 'Story on the Wind'. In Hebrew, it is called 'ruach' or the 'breath of God'.

GAINING A DEEPER RAPPORT WITH NATURE

What is most interesting about this great tide phenomenon is that it is perceivable in nature to all of us. If we quieten the noise in our minds just long enough, it can make itself evident. When we start to detect this rhythm, the tide can bring an amazing sense of connection with nature and we can feel that our senses are opening. We then gain a deeper rapport with the nature around us.

What is surprising is that when we connect to this tide, we can feel more connected with animals and birds. They can sometimes seem less instinctually fearful of us and may interact more. This sounds far-fetched but, really, it does start to happen: birds fly closer and wild animals come out of hiding. When we perceive this filed or tide, we often get a strong sense of being held by life. That is, we feel a deep support offered to us by the universe, a sense that our systems are more than just our psyche and physiology and that we are part of something much bigger than us but that we are intimately connected to it.

HEALING THE BODY

Within us, the tide can feel like it is healing the body, bringing about a sense of rebalance and restoration. You would think that we live within this great tide all the time. In reality, while nature does very much seem to be connected to this tide, it is as though we humans have become disconnected from it.

Children appear to maintain the connection, but as we grow older it seems to wane. I do not know why, but it may have something to do with its natural, slow rhythm. The breathing motion of this tide is quite slow, taking about ninety seconds to reach us from the horizon and return there. Maybe, as we grow up, we speed up our natural rhythm and in doing so lose this connection, like the Bushmen losing their connection to the wind when they entered the towns. What we really want to concentrate on here is learning to feel this tide and reconnect with it, which feels like the most natural thing in the world.

One of my biggest inspirations for writing this book occurred when, about ten years ago, I showed a woman on the Dynamics of Stillness course how to reconnect with the tide. Once she had experienced the feeling of it, she said that it wasn't just important to do this, but it felt like everybody's birthright. That struck me and inspired me to continue sharing what I have learnt, to help people reconnect with this most natural of phenomena.

Those who spend much time in nature can find it easier to perceive the tide compared to those who live in the city. It is possible that it comes down to there being far too much internal and external noise for us to sense freely – internal noise meaning constant mental activity and external noise meaning the constant bombardment of the senses by life. It is entirely possible to sense the tide in a city, in a deeply noisy or irritating situation, but this needs practise. To begin with, it is much easier to sense it in nature, and with a quiet mind.

The Great Tide

Begin the practice

Ideally, it is best to be in nature for this practice, but if you are in the city, position yourself, sitting, with a view of the horizon.

Start by aiming to access a little awareness of inner peace by trying to sense a degree of softness, fluidity and delicacy in your breathing.

Allow all your internal noise to quieten by not blocking anything. Allow the thoughts and feelings to occur, but gently bring your attention back to a sense of softness in your breath. Allow yourself to feel the sounds and smells around you. Let them come into your consciousness and then let them soften into the background.

Sense the stillness behind everything

Let your attention slowly move out towards the horizon and enjoy the sense that your awareness is there. Be fully aware of this.

Let your attention slip over the horizon

Letting your attention slip over the horizon will feel odd at first because, when you do this, you feel as though you are losing something for a second. Do not worry, your attention will return.

Let your attention return

Then, wait. Wait until you sense your attention being slowly returned to you. You could also sense a slow, mist-like fluid motion coming from the horizon towards you. You can't see this fluid motion, but you can sense it coming. This process takes a while – about a minute and a half. As the fluid motion approaches, it passes straight through you, undiminished, but you feel a subtle difference in sensation. You get the sense of feeling connected and infused and informed by this wind. It feels like it supports you and holds you and calms you.

Connect to everything living around you

The fluid motion, or tide, will then retreat back to the horizon, slowly, taking about fifty seconds. If you wait, the tide will return, in a slow, never-ending rhythm. It feels like it connects you to everything living around you. This awareness is difficult to achieve and you may not get it the first time. Just bring your awareness back to the softness in your breath, let your nervous system settle and gently try again. This feeling is subtle, but in the end all students on the course feel it and they do so in the same moment.

Conclusion

What is this great tide? Is it that we connect more deeply with the natural flows in nature? It's hard to explain, but it is evident and feels very connecting and healing.

As you practise this more and more, you can start to sense the tide coming in at certain quiet moments in the day. It may happen when there is a break in the constant action, or when you are doing a repeated rhythmic activity such as knitting or washing-up. The sense that you feel is that a gentle mist comes from the horizon and passes through you. It is a very subtle, fluid feeling.

So, if you keep your senses aware and open to your surroundings, and try to sense the stillness around you, you could connect more and more to the great tide and the amazing depth of riches it can bring.

CHAPTER 14

LETTING OUR SENSES BREATHE

Our senses are how we feel and interpret the world around us. They develop well before we are born. Touch/pressure, taste, vision, hearing and even some smell stimuli are received as soon as these sense organs develop in embryos. The 'wiring' of our brains at that time is simplistic, so our senses are not as advanced as they are today but they are developing and starting to function. Young babies respond to both pressure changes and sound in utero.

TOUCH

Recent research suggests that the parts of the brain that determine where we feel touch in the body produce a map that is formed by the embryo/foetus feeling its environment. At five weeks, embryos can sense touch on their nose and lips, and by twelve weeks, they can sense touch all over the body. A baby's first developed sense is touch, which is vital for bonding, feeding and aiding brain development. In newborn babies, the map is enhanced by early touch from the mother, father or other caregivers. The sensory map is at first diffuse, but as we grow it becomes sharply defined and has a close connection to our developing emotions.

Physical contact has been shown to be vital to growth and development. Touch reduces the reactivity of the body's stress systems and improves cognitive, emotional and immune function. I have spent many years treating orphans from Romania who, after birth, were left in cots with no physical contact. They would suffer limited or slower rates of growth, developmental delays and diminished immune and cognitive development.

A touch can be soothing, or it can be the opposite. As adults, if our touch sensors receive constant stimulation – for example, from the pressure of our clothes on our body – the brain becomes desensitized to these stimuli so we don't feel them as much. Some people with sensory developmental differences can often feel overwhelmed by their senses. As a young child, my daughter could not wear socks – she found the ridges of the seams too irritating so I had to send off to America for seamless socks. When we put on socks or shoes, our nervous systems learn to ignore the feeling of them after a while, but for my daughter, the feeling of her socks against her skin never stopped, it kept on nagging at her.

Our senses must desensitize us to certain stimuli. This is vital for life. The senses become desensitized when they are overstimulated. Since we live in a world of sensory overstimulation, our sensory awareness shuts down as a natural coping mechanism.

SMELL

Our ability to smell begins at around twenty-eight weeks in utero. Because of its location, the area of the brain that processes the sense of smell has a strong connection with the areas of the brain that focus on emotion and memory. Certain smells calm the foetus pre-birth. The smell of amniotic fluid has been shown to calm babies in the womb and the smell of the mother is important in helping babies bond. That maternal smell relates to a sense of nurture in our emotional makeup. Similarly, the smell of the father is linked to a sense of safety and comfort. Babies can discriminate smells nearly as well as adults, though their response is more direct – differing smells can directly affect their heart rate, breathing or aversion.

As we grow, our sense of smell links with certain deep emotions and memories. For example, the smell of a partner can affect us deeply. Women and girls have a stronger sense of this as the testosterone produced by boys and men blocks it to a degree. It is possible that this harks back to the days of the male hunter.

Our emotional experiences mean that we become conditioned to some smells and insensitive to others. Emotional stress can block our senses, especially the sense of smell. This patterning of the sense of smell in our memory and deeper emotions can be important in developing our Dynamics of Stillness work, as well as in developing our sensory awareness. Smell therapy and aromatherapy can have a direct impact on our emotions, bringing a sense of peace and calm.

TASTE

A much simpler sense than smell, though highly dependent upon it, taste can be divided into four categories: bitter, sour, sweet and salty. As we have discovered with our sense of smell, taste also connects closely with our emotions. The taste of amniotic fluid calms newborns. Babies can decipher all four categories of taste, but they prefer sweet. Sweet flavour receptors in the brain release opiates into the bloodstream, which are calming and bring pleasure. That is part of the reason why we like the taste of chocolate and why we tend to choose sweet things when we comfort eat.

VISION

Our sense of vision is primitive at birth. It is less important for bonding than the senses of touch, smell and taste. But our visual pathways in the brain wire up very quickly and by six months of age, our primary visual ability is in place: depth, colour, acuity and coordinated eye movement. Vision uses more processing space in the brain than our other senses combined.

As we grow, our brains learn to discriminate between the visual stimuli which is important and that which is background. We respond to changes in our environment and block out constant stimuli. In some ways this is necessary, otherwise our nervous systems would be constantly overwhelmed.

HEARING

A foetus in utero can hear from around the age of twenty-three weeks. It can hear its mother's voice and heartbeat, and can also discern other voices, such as that of the father and siblings. This hearing ability plays an important role in language development. Babies have been shown to prefer certain books that have been read to them in utero, along with certain music also played to them in the womb.

Our senses develop early and become the means by which we interpret our immediate environments and form responses in behaviours and emotions. On a preconscious level, we are reacting all the time to these stimuli without even being aware of it.

More than a thousand years ago, Taoist practitioners were aware of the importance of our senses and applied a variety of techniques to work in conjunction with them, especially in meditation and alchemy (we will talk in more detail about Taoist alchemy in Chapter 17, *see pages 88–9*).

In many Taoist meditation practices, the practitioners would start by 'closing down' their senses. This process was a way of bringing their sensory awareness back into their bodies. They would close their eyes and then try to shut down their hearing and other senses.

The Taoists were interested in the way we lose energy via our senses. They maintained that in order to successfully meditate, it was important to first return their senses back into their body.

In my work in teaching sensory development for practitioners, I am more interested in becoming conscious of where our senses are, meaning becoming conscious of exactly where we place our attention within the moment. If we can become conscious of our attention through our senses, we can learn to shift our attention at will, to optimize sensory awareness and to develop levels of stillness.

PRACTICE 14

Letting Your Senses Breathe

As you progress in your practice, it may seem as though you go over the same ground. There is a purpose to this. You are looking for a real change in your practice, in your sensory awareness and in your relationship to yourself and your health, and a stronger connection to the deep tides in nature. You are also developing a deepening relationship to stillness and, eventually, dynamic stillness, and with it, an increasing sense of wholeness and oneness – wholeness wherein you have a feeling of being complete and oneness wherein you have a feeling of being connected with everything around you, as an intricate part of the whole (*see pages 138–9*). This is a huge task and it takes time, like planting a seed and tending to the growing sapling daily. This cultivation, in my experience, brings wonderful results, but there is no fast path to sustained growth. The tending must be constant and consistent. Hopefully the journey will be fun, too.

Begin the practice

To begin this practice, sit comfortably (*see page 37*). For this session, you can be outdoors in nature or indoors. Either way, it is possible for your senses to be filled and emptied.

Bring awareness to your breath and do not judge it. Sense the stillness and quietness, or the potential for them, in your breath.

Bring awareness to your sense of touch

Once you begin to feel neutral and calm, you can bring your awareness to your sense of touch. Focus on the palms of your hands. If they are facing downwards on your legs or on the ground, turn your hands to face upwards, so your palms are not touching anything physical.

Bring awareness to the weight of the air

The weight becomes very real as you bring your attention to it. Enjoy the sense of the weight of the air on your palms and let your touch sense widen, as if you are holding up the air in the room or outside. Can you feel that? The feeling connects you to the room or, if you are outside, it connects you to the horizon.

Now, bring your awareness of touch back so it feels like it returns to you, back inside your body, and again there is nothing to feel in your hands. What I am interested in here is developing your ability to move your sensory awareness or attention at will.

Bring awareness to your vision

Try this again, this time with your vision. For this, it helps to have a horizon in view. Bring your visual awareness to your immediate surroundings and enjoy for a moment what is around you. Then let your visual awareness move slowly to the horizon, as if allowing the visual sense to breathe out to the horizon. Now, as you did with the great tide practice before (*see pages 70–1*), let your visual awareness drop over the horizon and wait in comfort, knowing your attention will return to you on the great tide.

Bring awareness to your hearing

Try this with your hearing. Start by listening to the immediate sounds in your environment, the sounds of your breathing or the background noises in the room. Now let your hearing expand to outside. Really let the sense breathe out, so you almost feel the outside world with your hearing. Now try to hear the stillness that is behind the noise. Can you hear it? It is always there.

CHAPTER 15

NATURE AND CONNECTION

As we have seen in recent chapters, our world is made up of a huge variety of interacting fluid tides. This is borne out by both modern science, including modern physics and cell biology, both tell stories of interacting fields from a cellular to a planetary level. The inherent knowledge of the indigenous tribes of the world talk of mankind being connected by a great tide or wind of God. It seems that our modern senses need to catch up with this understanding. Our practice is developing this, our sense awareness, with the hope that we will start to sense these fields and tides, which can open us up to a deeper level of connection and peace.

Over successive generations, through scientific discovery and agricultural and industrial revolutions, mankind has learnt to harness some of the elements in nature, to grow food to sustain the rapidly expanding population, to provide power to run homes and businesses, to make medicines and stem disease and to build homes. In doing so, we have lost that deeper connection with the natural rhythms in nature.

In medieval times, humans would hibernate in winter, stockpiling harvests, creating and sustaining warmth and curtailing activities as they endured the season's harshness. The story is very different now. At the local supermarkets we are able buy almost any food types at almost any time of the year; we can provide environments that feel like summer in midwinter, and vice versa.

LOSING CONTACT WITH THE NATURAL RHYTHMS

Through this dietary and environmental progression we have lost contact with the natural rhythms and how they affect our bodies throughout the year. Certain foods suit our bodies in different seasons. For example, in summer, lighter foods, fruits, salads and uncooked foods suit us better. In winter, however, warm soups and broths serve us well. Nowadays, there are popular fads for consuming cold smoothies made from raw veg and fruit at any time of year. This overburdens the natural process of our digestive system, which can cause digestive problems.

I am not craving romantically former times when there was no technology – I love technology – but I think we need to remain connected to nature's rhythms and tides, not only to maintain good health but to deepen the richness of our existence and become fully aware of the harm brought about by the loss of that connection.

These ideas are not new. Every day we hear from different sources that humans are destroying the earth. We become numb to these words, thinking that nothing can be done about global warming and the destruction of our environment. We hope that nature will adapt, or that future generations will discover new ways to ensure planetary survival. But is that enough?

WAKING UP TO NATURE

The deeper we connect with nature, the more conscious we become. One of my hopes with these practices is for us to wake up to nature and live more symbiotically with it, rather than unconsciously try to harness and control it.

We find nature everywhere. I am always surprised to discover, when in central London, the number of foxes moving among us, even in Trafalgar Square. I remember I would fly into London from Ireland on a Thursday evening to attend my practice in Harley Street each Friday. When I got off the tube, I would sit on a wall under some magnolia trees, with the Westway, one of London's busiest roads, just in front of me. I had come from the easy stillness

of my practice in the countryside of rural Tipperary into the heart of London and the noise was overwhelming. But I would sit under those beautiful trees and acknowledge what an amazing job they did, bringing beauty and stillness into the chaos. I would sit there for half an hour in the late evening, ignored by passers-by, and acclimatize to London, connecting to the underlying stillness behind all the noise. In the spring, the blossom on those trees was unsurpassed.

BUILDING OUR CONNECTION WITH NATURE

I want us, in this work, to start to build our connection with nature so we can learn to read its patterns, stories and tides. We are part of nature but we tend to forget that so easily.

Western belief systems have increased our disconnection from nature. Most of the world's religions position God as an outside force, which is different from the indigenous tribes who place Him in everything and see us humans as part of an interconnected whole. This philosophy of placing God as an outside force, coupled with our modern Western reductionist philosophy, which is based on rationality and logic rather than intuition, serves to dissociate us further from feeling a strong, clear and consistent connection with nature.

Technology, sensory overstimulation and city life take us even further away from our connection with nature. I am not saying that we should all start worshipping the earth, moon and stars as gods, but if we engage with the idea of accepting that everything is part of an interconnected One – which makes most sense to me, philosophically, scientifically and morally – it could help us to reconnect. If we place ourselves as an integral part of nature, it helps us to find a deeper connection with what is around us. This also helps us to connect with our own inner nature, which is more than our temperament, it is our instinct, which can be seen as an expression of our health.

Our practice here is to develop our connection to nature by going through the stages we know already – allowing our senses to slowly expand, to start detecting stillness in and around us, to start to feel fluid tides within and around us – and then start to contact and connect with these fields in nature.

In some of the older Taoist teachings from nearly a thousand years ago, there are many practices for engaging with different elements in nature and some beautiful techniques for connecting with and melding with them. After work, I go into the courtyard and practise a variety of processes and practices that I have discovered through ancient books and teachings. These bring a sense of connection with nature.

There is something beautiful about standing in the stillness of the night and connecting with the energy of the moon, or meeting the dawn sunrise, or feeling the gentle fields of trees and plants. I always teach these different examples of connection on the Dynamics of Stillness courses, allowing students to connect with the fields of trees and plants, and they really enjoy feeling these connections. The amazing thing is, if we meet nature with respect and gentle awareness, it seems that nature engages back.

I started to work with the natural energetics in plants in 2001, making flower essences very much in the same way as Dr Edward Bach when he created Bach Flower Remedies in the 1930s. I have made more than eighty essences from separate flowers and thirty combination essences. The key is to sense the energetic fields of the flowers and see how they interact with the energy fields of a person. Usually, I would get my children to hold a flower and I would try to read its effects on their fluid fields. It sounds odd, but the flower essences really are wonderful, gentle and supportive, and I have been using them for more than fifteen years now. I call them the Irish Wildflower Essences and they are available from my practice. I learnt to work with these essences by becoming better able to perceive these fields in nature. Working with the flower essences helps me connect more deeply with nature.

Nature and Connection

Begin the practice

For this practice you should ideally be outside in nature, in a garden or park. You are going to use a standing posture. If it is warm enough, it is lovely to do this practice with bare feet.

Relax into a standing posture

Stand facing a tree, plant, flower or shrub, ideally within touching distance. Place your feet shoulderwidth apart with your knees just slightly bent, arms at your sides and palms facing the ground.

Let your body relax into this standing posture. Feel your feet on the floor. Bring your attention to the mid-foot, just behind the ball of the foot. This point is K1 (kidney 1) in Taoism/Chinese medicine. From here, expend your awareness about 30 centimetres (12 inches) into the ground below your mid-foot and start to sense your connection to the earth. This is a lovely technique to do if you need to ground yourself, or if you have been doing a lot of work with your brain, such as studying. This brings you back into your body and 'earths' you.

Find your neutral and sense the quiet stillness around you

Now, repeat your usual practice of finding your neutral – by tuning into the softness of your breath, by accepting, allowing and observing thoughts, feelings and emotions. Then, when you are comfortable and quiet, try to get a sense of the quiet stillness behind the sounds around you.

Sense the fluidity within

From this point of neutrality, extend your arms to touch the tree, plant, flower or shrub. Touch it softly, almost as if your hands were transparent. Try to sense a fluidity with your hand. Is there any fluid movement up the tree? Can you feel this fluidity?

Feel the tree's energetic field

Take a step backwards so that your out-stretched hands are about 30 centimetres (12 inches) from the tree. I want you to see if you can feel the tree's energetic field. This is a subtle, energetic field you can feel with your hands.

There is a definite boundary to the field of the tree. The field of a plant is about 30 centimetres (12 inches) fully around it, but the field of a tree is much bigger – nearer 3 or 4 metres (10 or 13 feet) as the usual field boundary for a good-sized tree. Move back until you sense with your hands a change in density of the air around your hand. You will now be able to feel the boundary of the field of the tree. Repeat this with plants, rocks and other items in nature.

Conclusion

Feel a sense, as if there is a harmonizing of your fluid fields and those of the tree. It's like you and the tree are hugging and meeting. It feels wonderful! Do you feel a deeper connection with the tree?

CHAPTER 16

MASTERING ATTENTION

One of the most important elements that we are learning is firstly to become aware of, then to master, exactly where we place our attention at any given moment.

We have already started to learn to expand our attention to the stillness around us and the stillness on the horizon, and to sense stillness within us and in the environment around us. As we go on, we will learn to place specific, focused attention on elements within nature. We will also start to learn to place our attention in particular ways inside our body, learning to shift our attention from what feels blocked to what feels good, and in doing so, connect to the energy in our body that is working for its health. By tuning in to this vital expression of health, we go on to learn rudimentary healing techniques.

These steps allow us to focus and expand our attention, to let out attention be free, to move with the natural flow and dynamics of life, and then to focus our attention again when the timing is perfect for us to do so.

BECOMING CONSCIOUS OF WHERE OUR ATTENTION LIES

Here in our practice we are going to work to increase our attention *on* our attention, to become conscious of where our attention lies, from moment to moment. If we achieve this ability, the first thing it does is bring us directly into the moment. For example, when we become aware that our attention is on some past event or some future scenario, what happens? The very action of being aware of our attention brings our attention directly back to the moment – a clever trick, really, and so simple.

If we play a little with our attention, we can let it go wherever it wants in time and space: to a happy time back in the past, in a specific place, with a particular loved one. It is like part of us returns to that moment. If we bring conscious awareness to that moment, we remain connected to that time and place. This is an important element of developing a meditative practice. It does not matter where your mind goes, as long as you are conscious of it. You are brought back to the moment in a non-judgemental way and it actually feels good.

So the art of mastering our attention starts with becoming conscious to our attention, in a non-judgemental manner. Once we are conscious of our attention, we can then decide what to do with it; we can learn to shift it at will. If we can learn to master our attention, we can learn to focus it exactly where we want it in place, time and feeling. From this, we can access a whole world of possible ways to stop the anxiety and stress of modern life.

SOFTENING OUR FOCUS

The first step when becoming aware of our attention in the moment is to soften our focus just a little, so our attention can feel free to roam. When we are stressed and anxious it is important to free our attention so that we do not fixate on negative thoughts, feelings or emotions. To actively soften our grip on our attention, we actively softening our focus. Just allow it to soften with your mind – usually it works immediately when we try it. If not, keep at it and allow all the feelings that come up. If we practise the accepting, allowing and, finally, observing technique we learnt in Chapter 2 *(see pages 16–21)*, the process instantly works to loosen our grip on our attention.

Once our attention is free, we can learn to send it wherever we want, whenever we want. It helps us connect very deeply with whatever we place our attention on, especially in nature.

Mastering Attention

Begin the practice

Find a comfortable spot – in nature is best, but a view would be OK. Sit comfortably and allow your breathing to soften a little.

Become aware of where your attention is

Your attention could be with the work you were just doing or some domestic worry, or it might be on a future or past event. Wherever it is, bring your attention *to* your attention.

Soften your attention

Let your attention touch whatever it touches lightly, like a feather. It doesn't matter what you place your attention on – just accept, allow and observe, as you have learnt to do.

Place your attention on something visual

If you have a view outside, let your attention draw you to your visual environment. Remain conscious that you are placing your attention wherever you are.

Place your attention on your hearing

Let your attention pick up whatever it can – remaining conscious that you are placing your attention on your hearing.

Place your attention on a good memory

Allow your mind's eye to visualize a good memory. Become aware of the sounds, smells and images, and also the feelings of this memory, while also maintaining awareness, that you are doing this.

Project your attention into the future

Place your attention on something you are looking forward to. Try to bring in the senses again – the visuals, the sounds and the smells of it (*see pages 76–7*). While you do this, keep a little of your attention on the fact that you are doing this.

Conclusion

By maintaining awareness of where your attention is, and keeping it as light as a feather, you can learn to become a master of your attention, allowing it to feel free, while learning to place it with precision wherever you wish it to be.

CHAPTER 17

LCHEMY

We have focused on fluidity, on the great tides of nature, on the story on the wind and we have started to open our senses to this gentle, fluid motion. These are steps in our sensory and perceptual development. We are now going to turn our awareness towards sensing where motion arises. The motion we feel can be traced back to a source, which is stillness. We will try to feel this stillness, be it in a place or perception.

I have long been interested in alchemy. It is a complex subject, but at its core is the process of transmutation, which is turning one form of matter into another, such as lead into gold.

Alchemy can be thought of as both a philosophy and a practice, which can be looked at on many levels. It is a process that has been in existence for almost 4,000 years, having been developed in three main regions – Taoist China, India and the West. Western alchemy is thought to have come from Egypt, with the city of Alexandria being the centre of alchemical knowledge. From Egypt it travelled to the Islamic world, then finally to Europe.

The aims of alchemy have been twofold. The first, the physical transmutation, is known as exoteric alchemy ('exo' means external, linking to physical transformation). This external alchemy involved the purification and perfecting of the physical characteristics of certain objects, especially base metals, which could lead to, for example, turning lead into gold. Exoteric alchemy was also focused on creating an elixir of immortality, also called the philosopher's stone.

The second aspect of alchemy, esoteric alchemy ('eso' meaning internal), was about an inner transmutation of the spirit, which involved internal purification to a more enlightened state of being.

Many historians believe that one form of alchemy cannot be separated from the other and even that the exoteric was a metaphor for an inner transformation.

My understanding of Taoist esoteric alchemy comes from writings from the Song dynasty in the fourteenth century, notably from the Quanzhen (*Way of Complete Perfection* or *All Truth Religion*) branch of Taoism. The first level of Taoist esoteric work was the ingesting of certain substances for the process of spiritual development. The second level concerned itself with the internal transmutation of energy.

A PLACE WHERE MOTIONS ARISE FROM STILLNESS

What interests me here is the third level for esoteric, internal alchemy, as practised by the Taoists of some of the Quanzhen schools. The third level, or process, describes a somewhat deeper process, which links very much with our developing practice. It involves sitting in a meditative posture and finding the place where motion arises from stillness. In some texts this energy centre – the dan tien – typically has a location at a place just below the umbilicus, while in other texts it is described as a place behind the mid-brow. Other schools and masters say there is no location for the dan tien, just a feeling-sense quality.

In alchemical Taoism, the dan tien is called the opening, the place from which movement arises, where the manifest arises from the unmanifest. In Taoism, the Tao is both the manifest and the unmanifest, the absolute principle underlying all things, combinging within itself the code of human conduct in harmony within the natural order. But an important part of practice development in Taoism is to learn to wait at the opening, at this place from which movement arises.

These alchemical practices have a relevance to what we are doing in this Dynamics of Stillness course. By cultivating and practising techniques steadily and repeatedly, our practice deepens in many subtle ways. First, the practice becomes easier to do. Then, as we practise, we can start to enter these states at will, more and more easily.

The jump to introducing alchemical practices of motion into our techniques may seem difficlt, but we already have a strong foundation of skills. We can by now bring our mind to a neutral place; we are starting to feel the tides in and around us, and we have begun to feel the stillness behind everything. We are going to put all this together and find the transition point between stillness and motion, and try to maintain an awareness of this place or feeling.

This chapter's practice can be achieved in many ways, but I will mention two for now. The first is to develop our practice of connecting to the great tide by sending out our awareness to the horizon, as we did in Chapter 13 (*see pages 70–1*). This time, though, we are allowing our awareness to rest lightly by waiting at the stillness on the horizon, keeping a sense of awareness there, even when the great tide moves in and out. In doing so, we are splitting our awareness to feel both the slow tidal motion of the great tide while simultaneously keeping an awareness on the stillness at or beyond the horizon.

SPLITTING OUR ATTENTION

I am asking that we do something new here – this idea of splitting our attention. If we think about it, though, this is something we do all the time. We can have an awareness of many things at once, such as tasting food while hearing music. But, here, we are going to split our attention within the feeling, or sensing, world that we are developing. I will elaborate on this in the following practice.

The second way to achieve this chapter's practice is to sit quietly and to start to feel a degree of internal fluidity. This can be anywhere inside or around us. From here, find the stillness that is behind the motion and, again, to sense both stillness and fluidity at the same time. Once you start to feel both, try to sense the place where stillness meets motion, or the place where motion arises from stillness. I often find this easier to do by sensing the underlying stillness that is everywhere, including inside me, while watching my internal fluid fields breathe. Then, sensing the place where they meet or, more accurately, where motion arises from stillness. I will develop this again in the two-part practice on the following pages.

Where Motion Arises from Stillness

PART 1: Begin the practice

For this practice you will need sit with a view towards the horizon. Start by sitting comfortably and going through the familiar process of finding neutral, allowing your mind to breathe as it releases its grip on your senses.

Expand your visual awareness

When you are comfortable and calm, allow your visual awareness to slowly and naturally expand to the horizon and, as you have done previously, just let your awareness drop over the horizon.

Open your feeling sense

Open your feeling sense to the quality of stillness that is present at the horizon or over the horizon. Enjoy the sense of peace and stillness. Soon you should start to get a sense of the tide moving very slowly, like a quiet cloud from the horizon.

Split your awareness

Now, split your awareness so that part of you is watching the motion and part of you is with the stillness it comes from.

PART 2: Begin the practice

You can be anywhere. Sit comfortably and quietly, and focus on the softness in your breath. By allowing, accepting and observing, your nervous system will naturally quieten to a feeling of neutral.

Move your attention to your fluid body

Allow your attention to be moved to something that feels fluid in your body. The fluidity is a freedom of motion and implies movement. Your body acts like one unit of fluid, which is softly breathing at a slow rate, much slower than your respiratory breathing, more like two to three cycles per minute. It is a soft, gentle breathing which is being expressed in each cell of your body.

Sense the motion that arises from stillness

Allow your awareness to take in the natural stillness that lies behind this fluid, breathing motion. Can you sense both stillness and the fluid breathing at the same time, or the place where the fluid motion arises out of stillness? It is not in a location, it is a felt-sense, a quality of feeling. If you don't feel it straight away, you soon will.

$\mathcal{F}$ULCRUMS

There are two English definitions of the word 'fulcrum'. The first, from physics, defines it as the point at which something is balancing or supported. The second definition describes it as the main thing or person needed to support something or make something work or happen. For our purposes, both definitions are relevant.

Fulcrums are things we can learn to feel with our developing felt-sense. What I am interested in here is that we start to get a felt-sense of fulcrums, both in and around our bodies. When it comes to fulcrums that we can feel around us, we need to start focusing our senses – particularly our feeling sense that we have been working with – and become aware of where the fulcrums are in relation to us, whether near or far.

SENSING ENERGY

I will give you an example of this. Every morning, when I wake up, the first thing I do is sense my energy and feel whether any of it is not in me. Our energy can be dragged off in many directions, through thoughts, dreams, feelings and emotional connections. Other factors can also affect how our energy is dispersed. If my feelings are with my partner or my children and we are apart, this often draws my energy away from me. When we become aware of where our energy is, however, something magic happen, the energy comes back as if of its own accord.

When I am teaching a course, the first thing I do is see if everybody has arrived. Here, I am looking to see if their energy is with them, or if it is still partly with their families, or still on the commute it took to get to the course, or in their thinking. I literally make sure they have completely arrived. An interesting anecdote about this idea is when, in the 1950s, a group of Native Americans flew by aeroplane to visit some dignitaries in London. The plane arrived at Heathrow, but none of the Native Americans moved a muscle. When asked why, they replied that they were waiting for their spirits to catch up. And sometimes it feels like this. Remember, we live in a quantum world where everything consists of packages of energy that resonate and relate to one another and where distance is irrelevant. If we think right now about a loved one, we send some energy towards them. When we have many things to think, worry and concern ourselves with, this can be very tiring.

BALANCING POINTS BETWEEN OURSELVES, OBJECTS, PEOPLE OR THOUGHTS

I am suggesting here that we have fulcrums in and around us for a great many things. These fulcrums are balance points between ourselves and the object, person or thought in question. We can also send our energy back in time by engaging with a memory. Likewise, we can direct our energy into the future by thinking about possible future events and ideas. Other factors can produce fulcrums that we can learn to feel in and around us and others.

When teaching osteopaths to develop their perception and palpation skills (examining areas of the body by a sense of touch and pressure), I teach them to start to feel these fulcrums in other people, which can affect the body by creating sensations of pulls and drags, in and around it.

THE MIDLINE FULCRUM

A midline is a central fulcrum, which can act like a centre of gravity in the body. If a patient has suffered an accident or a shock, they shift their entire midline to a new place. For example, if someone suffers a road traffic accident and is hit from behind, their midline fulcrum can move from inside the centre of their body to a place in front of them. The same thing happens with someone who is in shock.

A dramatic example of this happened while I was helping a colleague treat a patient. I knew nothing about the patient or his history, but as soon as I tuned in to him, I could see a strong midline fulcrum down to the side of the plinth he was lying on. He and I both acknowledged it and then something dramatic happened. The patient nearly fell off the table and almost passing out. Then he slowly came around and my friend put a blanket round him. When he had recovered, the patient told us his story. He was a coffee producer from Africa. One day he had an accident in his jeep, which had veered off the road and turned over, going down a steep embankment. He had woken up in a hospital. This accident had created a shock that had moved his midline fulcrum.

The amazing thing was that as he came to, he said, 'I'm feeling completely different.' All the pains in his head, neck and back had immediately disappeared. He placed a wad of cash on the table and walked out, and we never saw him again. The act of acknowledging the misalignment of his fulcrum was enough to trigger the self-healing.

AWARENESS OF FULCRUMS

The example above emphasizes the importance of becoming aware of these fulcrums, in and around us. The treatment for the coffee producer consisted of nothing more than an awareness of the fulcrum and this had a powerful effect on him.

In my view, energetic fulcrums can affect us in many different ways. They can be thoughts, feelings or sensations; they may be physical, affecting our posture and gait; they can be nutritional or the effect of an illness, accident or operation; or they can be relational, meaning these fulcrums can relate to people we are intimately connected to – family, friends or work colleagues. Whether they are positive or negative experiences, all of them disperse our energies in small or large ways and in various directions. Sometimes, if we are overwhelmed, our energies feel as if they have been scattered to the winds.

If, though, we can start to become aware of these fulcrums, or energetic drains, which affect us in so many different ways, we can bring these fulcrums together and stop our energy dispersing and draining away from us.

Again, as with the previously described example, all we need to do is become aware of these fulcrums and something magic can happen. The fulcrums change and those little packets of energy return to us. However, it takes sensitivity and a degree of awareness to be able to feel these fulcrums.

Now, we have some awareness of what a fulcrum is and we can develop our sensitivity to them. The key here is not to be concerned with these fulcrums. To develop our practice, we allow, accept and observe as before. In so doing, we are returning our energy back into our body. Just the simple sensing and acknowledging of these fulcrums is enough, we do not have to do anything else.

If we regard our body as a field of energy, if that energy is being drawn in many directions, it can literally tire us out so any meditative practice really needs to start with allowing all the energy to return to us. Once it has returned, the practices become much, much easier. The key is conscious awareness and this begins with the simple fact of knowing that we have fulcrums, or draws of energy, away from our centre. Then, precisely by acknowledging these fulcrums, they return to us, restoring our energy.

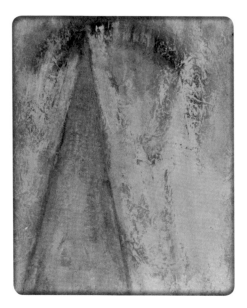

Fulcrums

Begin the practice

As I said, I like to do this when I first wake up, but you can do it anytime. Here, you do not need to use the neutral or stillness of tide practices – you can use this technique to restore your energy and bring you back to neutral before doing anything else.

Sense yourself as a fluid body

Start this practice either seated or lying down, whichever is most comfortable. Now, get a sense of yourself as a body contained within skin. Try to sense yourself as a fluid body, which is slowly breathing. From this, ask your body if any of your fluid energy is not inside you. A strange concept, but don't overthink – just use this felt-sense and feel your way through. Are you losing energy from your body? Can you get a sense of your energy self?

Sense how your energy responds to different thoughts

Think for a second about your favourite place, somewhere you love to be that makes you happy. Watch how your energy responds. Does some of it go to that place? Try to feel the movement. Now think about a loved one and this time really picture them as if they are right in front of you. Can you feel your energy move in front of you, as if going towards that person?

See the fulcrums

Try to see if you can feel these energy pulls and see the fulcrums. A fulcrum can be anything – a person, a feeling, time or a sensation – it really doesn't matter. This felt-sense takes time to achieve, but once you start to feel these pulls and fulcrums, it will become very, very clear.

Feel your lost energy return

Now, allow the fulcrum to be there and do not react. You may be able to feel what it is or where it comes from and you may not; it doesn't matter. What does matter is that you just allow and observe it. When you do this, a magical thing happens. The fulcrum shifts and that piece of lost energy returns to you. It's yours and nobody else's. This could be in the form of a thought, feeling, sensation or something more concrete, like a dragging feeling through your body caused by a fall or accident. Allow these sensations to be there while maintaining an awareness that you have a quiet, still centre.

Conclusion

This is a very subtle exercise that, as with everything else here, takes time to perfect. I assure you, though, once you get the sensation you will find it helpful, especially in situations where someone or something is draining you. Apply this practice and allow your energy to return to you. It will not have a negative effect on other people, it is your energy returning to you. In fact, when your energy is restored, it will help others. Also, remember that energy in the universe is limitless and, as you are an integral part of the universe, your energy is limitless too.

CHAPTER 19

THE FIRE OF IGNITION

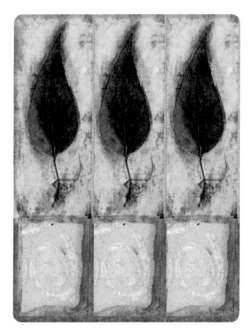

In my work as an osteopath, I teach the process of ignition. It is a fascinating concept. We would say that ignition in the physiology of the body implies that there is some sort of potency in the body's tissues. This seems to be an important prerequisite for health and the ability of the body to regulate, rebalance and heal itself.

The term 'ignition' is an act of setting something alight. It implies the use of light and fire, and the process of creating some combustion with other substances. An interesting manifestation of ignition, for me, is the presence of light behind the eyes. If we look into the eyes of someone who is happy, healthy, inspired or even in love, they tend to look radiant, as though their eyes are alight. In contrast, if you look into the eyes of someone who is tired, grieving or unwell, there is a definite absence of light. In my view, this is an outer manifestation of ignition.

WHERE THERE IS NO LIGHT, THERE IS NO LIFE

Put very simply, ignition implies light and light implies life. Where there is no light, there is no life. Without sunlight, the planet would freeze and nothing would grow – there would, literally, be no life. All life needs light. Ignition implies the presence of light within. It means our internal body has connected with the presence of light.

This concept has been used in many ways. One example is when we think of something new and exciting, and we describe having 'a light-bulb moment'. When we fall in love, we can feel as if we are 'basking in the light of love'; we literally shine like a light when we are in love and everybody sees it. Another example is our journey of birth, which is a passage from the darkness of the womb into the light. Similarly, when dawn breaks after the darkest moments of the night, it is like a slow and gentle ignition, waking up nature to the day.

In developing our Dynamics of Stillness practice, we can apply specific techniques to stimulate and enhance this ignition, which is vital when treating someone whose immune system is low, or someone who is very tired or grieving.

There was a practitioner who became a student of mine a few years ago. On arrival after hours of travel to see me at the practice, she told me, 'I had to visit because I have seen children treated by you and they have this wonderful light in their eyes.' I told her it was not some magic but just a technique and, fortunately, I could teach it to her.

Without the light of ignition, we are not 'firing on all cylinders'. This is the case, whether we are in the darkness of grief and loss or just plain tired and uninspired. Without ignition, it is hard to do even the basics of life and everything becomes a struggle, our immune systems are low, we easily catch various illnesses and can be depressed, down or unhappy.

BE AWAKE TO LIFE

We all need the light of ignition, which acts as a potent 'aliveness' within each cell in our body. It enlightens us, wakes us up to life, connects and energizes us. Is it possible to access this ignition and reconnect with it at will? I think so, but it demands certain prerequisites. It is much easier to connect with when we are well, happy and in nature, but once we learn how to connect, we can apply this practice when we are feeling low and down or below par healthwise.

PRACTICE 19

Ignition

Begin the practice

The first thing you need to do here – and it is vital for this practice – is to accept

exactly how you are feeling. At first, try this practice when you are healthy and happy, but once you get the idea, you can try it when you are tired or low. Allow and accept exactly how you are. Now bring your awareness to the softness in your breath. Really sense something delicate that feels sweet and soft.

Initially, try this practice in nature, but after a while you can do it anywhere. It is a little like the technique for the great tide in Chapter 13 (*see pages 70–1*) but there is an important difference. Here, we are going to sense a quality of light within the tide.

When your nervous system becomes a little quiet and you are feeling calm and comfortable, your thoughts will start to slow down. Only observe them if they arise, so they can fall away just as easily.

Open your sensory awareness

Let your sense of vision open and breathe out as far as the horizon. Allow it to go over the horizon and meet something that feels still. Let your sensory awareness be open to sensing a stillness at and beyond the horizon. Wait until you get that sense of the great tide arising from that stillness moving slowly towards you.

Sense a quality of light

At this point, tune into your sensory awareness. Try to sense a quality of light within this tide. It is there and if you open your awareness, it can feel light. Let this light tide, with its quality of brightness, flow and pass through you.

Conclusion

Allow the tide to awaken a sense of light in every cell of your body. It feels truly wonderful, doesn't it? The tide wakes up the body's connection to the element of light. The effect is that of an ignition; it can literally light us up. Once you feel this, go and look in the mirror and see how light your eyes are.

CHAPTER 20

HEALING BREATH

Breathing, as we have already found, is an important part of practice (*see page 66*). In this chapter we will start to explore the healing potential within our breath. This is the beginning of a deeper process in our practice, which will start to look at methods of self-healing and self-care. If we start with our breath, we can begin to learn to rebalance our body and mind in a very gentle and supportive manner.

In many Eastern religions and practices, including Hinduism, yoga, Taoism and Buddhist meditation, there is an emphasis on breathing. In Taoist practice, the breath is thought to be sitting at the threshold between the physical and energy bodies. Taoist philosophy looks at the movement of energy – known as *qi* (pronounced 'chee') – through specific channels called meridians that run within and around the body. They believe that if the energy channels remain fluid and free, without stagnation, health will be maintained. Stagnancy, in their view, causes illness. They use specific breathing techniques to help move the *qi* freely in the meridians. Yoga practice pays a lot of attention to the breath. Breathing can be calming, re-energizing and, according to Kriya Yoga, spiritually transformative.

In physical terms, our breathing can reveal a lot about our health and it can betray our emotional state, too. If we are distressed, we often breathe fast and our breathing becomes shallow and laboured. When we are relaxed and calm, our breath is usually slow and steady. If we are unwell, suffering with a fever, for example, our breathing can be fast and irregular. It is clear that our breathing reacts to the state of our mind and body. So maybe, if we reverse our thinking and take positive action on our breathing, we can use it to affect the state of our body and mind.

BRINGING AWARENESS TO OUR BREATHING

In Taoist Sung breathing – Sung meaning relaxed or when tension is transferred from the physical body to the energetic realm – the emphasis is on bringing awareness to our breathing and then directing our breath to those areas of the body that are suffering from tension and distress. This positive breathing activity is intended to soften and calm the body.

As I have already mentioned, when we don't breathe effectively, our bodies suffer. Tension, whether physical, mental or emotional, builds up in a variety of ways. First, it can tighten up our bodies and certain muscle groups, such as our shoulders, back muscles, legs, pelvic muscles and, especially, our diaphragm, the big breathing muscle that sits as a dome shape at the bottom of our ribs. When we are tense and our breathing has become tight, this diaphragm muscle contracts, which further constricts our breathing.

We must learn two new skills for this practice. The first is to bring our awareness, attention and finally intention to specific parts of the body, and from there to bring our awareness, attention and finally intention to our thoughts, feelings and emotions. The second skill follows closely on from the first and involves bringing – via our intention – our breath first to specific areas of the body, and then to our thoughts, feelings and emotions.

This two-part practice sounds a little complex, but if we break it down, it is quite easy to do. It just requires us to become aware of and able to direct our attention quite specifically. This sounds rather an odd thing to do, to breathe into certain parts of the body, but if we use our newly developing felt-sense, it is easier than you would think. The purpose of using our intention and attention to bring our breath to specific areas of our body that require consideration, is that we are going to use our breath to help change these specific areas. For example, my lower back is sore now. I am writing, perched on a stool with bad posture. But if I start to breathe deeply, as if breathing into my lower back, I can breathe the quality of softness into it. As I exhale, I release the accumulated tension in my lower back and it is already beginning to feel better.

There is a little trick to make sure this works. Within any sore or blocked part of us, there is some fluidity in the block, albeit often the tiniest speck. This feels like a tiny, sweet softness that is present within the block. If we breathe in softness to meet that tiniest softness already present within the block, something wonderful happens. That tiny speck of softness expands and grows – it can feel warm, soft and fluid, as if releasing the block. So, I breathe into the block and it releases easily. OK, it was only a minor twinge, but, as with all the skills we are cultivating, the more we develop our skill base, the more powerful the response will be to the practices.

This practice is easiest to do at first if we bring awareness to specific body parts and release the accumulated tension in them. However, with practice and increased self-awareness, we can also bring this healing breath to feelings, thoughts and emotions. The key to this technique is to develop an increased sensitivity to and awareness of how and what we are feeling. When we start to feel areas in our body that are not just sore but blocked, or simply not as full of vitality as they should be, we can start to work to release the blocks and difficult areas. The trickier bit, of course, is applying this technique to our thoughts, feelings and emotions, as we can often find it difficult to articulate how we are feeling. But we can use this time in our practice to check in with our thoughts, feelings and emotions. The clearer we can become about what our blocks are, the more we can access ways to breathe in softness and breathe out the tensions and let them go.

Healing Breath

Begin the practice

It would be helpful if you can allow yourself ten to fifteen minutes of time for this practice.

Start this practice by sitting comfortably. Then, check in to see how you are feeling. This is a good habit to get in to. On the physical side, get a sense of your body. Are there any aches, pains or sore spots?

Now look a little deeper. Start with your feet. Is anything blocked, tight or uncomfortable? Take note for now. Move up to your legs, pelvis, stomach, lower back and the rest of your spine. Take your time on this, noting any sore parts and potential blocks. Now focus on your chest, then your throat, neck, face, head and eyes.

Access your feelings

Are you happy, sad or feeling nothing much at all? Do you have any lingering thoughts, any feelings? Just take note for now that they are here. The more you do this, the better and more precise you will get at it. Hopefully, you now have a list of aches, spots, blocks and thoughts that you have noticed in your body.

Great! It's now time to build your tools.

Tune into your breath

Don't take deep breaths, keep them shallow while you then meet something soft and sweet in your breath. Then, start your usual practice of accepting and allowing any thoughts, feelings and emotions that come to mind, but this time you will do something different with your thoughts, feelings and emotions.

Feel your thoughts, feelings and emotions

If a thought, feeling or emotion comes up, try to fully allow yourself to feel it. As you open up to that thought feeling or emotion, breathe your soft, sweet breath into that feeling, allowing the sweetness in the breath to penetrate the feeling of that thought, emotion or feeling. It does not matter if the feeling is positive or negative, just breathe softness into it. As you breathe out, let the feeling release from you and your body.

Usually there are three or four layers of thoughts, feelings and emotions to work through, so you need to repeat this technique until your mind naturally gets a little quiet. You will know you have reached this point when your breathing softens more and you feel quite balanced.

Let your awareness and attention rest on the blocked places in your body

Now bring your awareness to the first body ache, pain or sore spot on your list. Really let your awareness and attention rest at the blocked place in your body. Now try to become more precise and detailed in your attention, in the soreness. In the block there is always a tiny bit that shows a little softness or fluidity. If you cannot find that spot of fluidity, look more precisely. It could literally be the size of a pinhead. Once you find this little sense of fluidity in the pain or block, start to breathe in that softness to meet the fluidity in the block. As you exhale, let the block and tension release and physically breathe it out. Then breathe in softness and exhale tension.

Sometimes you cannot feel any fluidity in the block, especially if the pain is severe. If that's the case, try to access the idea that there could be some softness and a little fluidity in the pain. Remember to physically breathe out the tension as you exhale. If you still cannot find any softness in the pain or block to meet with your soft breath, then spend a few minutes breathing softness into the block and breathing out tension. After a minute or two of this, you should be able to access a little part of the pain or block that has some soft fluidity to it.

Conclusion

As your sweet, soft breath meets the inherent softness in the block or pain, a magic thing happens. The softness in the pain increases and the pain softens and decreases. It is as if you are accessing the potential for health inside the block and, as you access this, it transforms the block.

This is a very important step in your practice as you are starting to find the underlying capacity for health in your problem areas. As you do so, you will start to access a deep process of self-healing. You will build more on this idea of self-healing in later chapters.

CHAPTER 21

CONNECTING HEAVEN AND EARTH

In classical Taoism, everything in the universe is considered as an interaction between two energies, Yin and Yang. Yin is earth energy, the feminine, stillness, internal and quiet. Yang is creativity, activity, heaven, the male, action and change.

In the Taoist view of creation, there was an original state of absolute oneness, called Wuji.This state is a point of stillness, the unmanifest Tao. The seed from whence everything manifest comes,it has no location and is everywhere.

YIN AND YANG

From the stillness of Wuji arose two energies: Yin – the denser, quieter earth energy – and Yang – the light expression of creation, the heavens. Yin and Yang are polar opposites. The ancient Taoists perceived all life in its manifest form as different interactions between these two polar energies. The intertwining energies were the qi, which, as we know *(see page 101)*, is a vibrational force of energy that moves everything in the universe. The Taoists connected the lighter, more heavenly energies of Yang with our consciousness, or spirit, and psyche, while the Yin energy was connected more of the earth, dark and dense.

It can be confusing to look at the energies of Yin and Yang as female and male, which is how they are often interpreted. That was not how the Taoists saw them, and would say that a man and a woman each hold feminine and masculine yin and yang energies and qualities. They referred to feminine, in terms of Yin, as internal, still, dark, earth-like energy, with Yang being the polar opposite as creative expression and action. A person has both energies to varying degrees. The denser the energy of Yin, the more 'of the earth' and physical the person is. Humans are considered to be the meeting point of the two polar energies of Yin and Yang. From a Taoist viewpoint, our energy is constantly changing and fluctuating between these two opposites.

The Taoists were looking to harmonize these Yin and Yang poles to bring the practitioner closer and closer towards the state of Wuji, the unmanifest stillness before the polarity of Yin and Yang. The Taoists considered this to be the ultimate goal of cultivational practice.

Taoist practitioners (*see also esoteric alchemy, page 88*) practised refining energy within the body in order to lighten the heavier, earth-connected Jing energy to Shen, the closest to what could be considered heavenly, pure Yang energy. This process of transformation of the heavy to light energy is a key element in many Taoists practices. The internal cultivation of energy was a spiritual process, which served to connect practitioners to the earthly and the celestial – and to connect these two energies. This was part of a process of internal cultivation that was important to Taoist practices.

It is an interesting and potentially transformative practice to learn to feel the Yang and Yin energies of heaven and earth, and to allow them to meet and connect within our body. Calming and energizing, it enables us to feel deeply connected to our surrounds, nature and the universe.

The Yin and Yang energies each have a specific quality that can be felt within our developing sensory awareness. The Yang energy is light and subtle, whereas the Yin energy is dark and rich. There are various places in the body in which to feel this meeting of heaven and earth. I prefer allowing the two energies to meet in my lower abdomen, a couple of inches below my umbilicus. It feels very natural there and this location was used by Taoist practitioners, who called it dan tien (*see page 88*).

Connecting Heaven and Earth

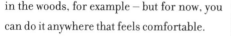

Begin the practice

Ideally, it is best for this two-stage practice to be done outdoors in nature – in your garden or by a stream in the woods, for example – but for now, you can do it anywhere that feels comfortable.

Adopt a standing posture for this technique – unless you have knee problems, in which case try it sitting down (*see page 37*). Stand with your feet shoulder-width apart and your hands at your sides. Now bend your knees a little and drop your pelvis – this helps to straighten the spine.

Allow your legs to relax and your spine to lengthen. Drop your chin down to allow some space in your upper neck. Let your shoulders soften and relax. This position should feel comfortable.

Bring your attention to the softness in your breath, using the allow, accept and observe tools (*see pages 16–21*). Bring your awareness to the fluidity within your body. Once you are feeling comfortable and neutral, you can begin the first stage of this connection practice.

Stage 1: Heaven Yang

Lift your hands to just above waist level, slightly in front of you, and turn your palms so they are facing the heavens. As you breathe in, expand your awareness to the sky. Use your sensory perception to feel a light, delicate energy. It helps if it is sunny as the sun's energy is similar to the energy you are trying to feel in your body. However, this energy is more than the sun; it feels like the sun, the stars and the heavens combined. It is just as easy to feel this energy at night.

As you breathe in, allow the light, sun and star energy to come into your body through your head and the palms of your hands and into your lower stomach. As you breathe out, just relax and let your tensions go. With each in-breath, feel more connection to this light energy. The main sensation will be a sense of welling, a soft fluid warm feeling in your lower stomach, but you will feel it from head to toe. It is very similar to the ignition energy you felt in Chapter 19 (*see page 100*). It feels light and peaceful.

Spend four to five breaths letting your body feel as if it is breathing in the light energy. It is, though, more than breathing through your lungs: it is as if every pore is filling with light, gentle, heavenly Yang.

Once you feel a strong connection with this Yang energy and a welling of warmth in your lower stomach, move to the second stage of this practice.

Stage 2: Earth Yin

Keep your arms in the same position but this time turn the palms of your hands to face downwards, towards the earth. I like to get a sense of the earth and its energy first. It is not light, like the heavenly energy, but delicate, strong and equally peaceful, with a deeper quality of feeling.

Expand your awareness, first, to a point about 30 centimetres (12 inches) below your feet. Really feel the connection to the earth. As you breathe in, allow the Yin energy of the earth to rise up through the mid-sole of your feet and into your lower stomach. As you breathe out, let go and allow the energy to move back down through the soles of your feet into the earth. This is a wonderfully grounding, energizing feeling, especially helpful in releasing your tension into the earth with each out-breath. Continue this stage until you feel energized, connected, and have released all your tensions.

Stage 3: Combining Heaven and Earth

For this final stage, you are going to bring your hands into a more neutral position, facing the front of the lower stomach. Keep your fingers relaxed and comfortable, and your arms raised slightly. Now imagine you are holding a large ball in front of you.

At this point, you are going to split your attention in two directions as you combine the two stages together. On your in-breath, breathe in from above and below – both heaven and earth – at the same time, drawing in both energies until they meet beautifully and delicately in front of your lower stomach. The feeling is energizing and peaceful as the two different qualities meet in your lower stomach and blend into a delicate energy that holds both elements. This can be hard to feel at the beginning, but it gets easier each time you do it.

My usual morning routine starts with running and stretching, followed by this standing practice, which I find invaluable for its ability to rebalance, reconnect and energize me. It leads naturally to connecting with the great tide (*see pages 70–1*) and other stillness practices.

SECTION

III

HEALING
and SENSING

CHAPTER 22

DYNAMIC STILLNESS

When you think about the phrase 'dynamics of stillness' does it make sense? Stillness is defined as a lack of motion, so how does this phrase have meaning? How can there be a dynamic within stillness? That is what we will explore in this chapter.

Previously, we looked at the Taoist concept of Wuji (*see page 106*), the unmanifest Tao or unified energy from which arises the manifest, or creation and form. But by its nature, Wuji has the potential from which all motion manifests.

In our practice so far, when we have started to experience stillness – for example, in Chapter 7 (*see pages 39–41*) – we have felt it imbued with a sense of potency, like a potential energy. As we develop our relationship with the stillness around and inside us, we will start to sense differing qualities within it.

EXPERIENCING DYNAMIC STILLNESS

When I am teaching palpation (examining areas of the body by a sene of touch or pressure) and sensory awareness to my colleagues, we encounter a quality that we call dynamic stillness, which can be felt when we sense the great or long tide and the way its slow, breathing motion is palpable in the body. From this point if the practitioner shifts their attention to meet the stillness from which the tide arises, it is as if they move through a perceptual doorway. This is a very light, almost translucent quality of stillness, which has a quiet but great power.

This dynamic stillness has a fascinating quality. It feels continuous, meaning it feels like the body of the patient dissolves into the stillness and becomes translucent and without form. When we are treating a patient and we wait with this light quality of dynamic stillness, an interesting thing happens. It feels as though the body of the patient starts to reform, as though it is re-creating itself. It's a wonderfully peaceful feeling for both patient and practitioner. This sensory experience is quite common when treating patients. It can be induced as described above or it can happen spontaneously. Of course, the patient does not dissolve into light, but they can feel certain phenomena happening to themselves. When I first had this treatment applied to me, it felt as if I was floating just a couple of inches above the table. I wasn't, of course, but I felt rather free and very peaceful.

My understanding of dynamic stillness has been acquired through years of feeling it, especially when I have been working on patients. I have also felt it when I have been doing sitting practices of meditation. When this quality of dynamic stillness appears, it feels as though the boundary between me and the universe dissolves, and I am totally part of a perfect oneness with the universe. This is dynamic stillness. The feelings of peace, oneness and connection are difficult to describe without experiencing them. It is wonderful! And I think this quality must be like the Wuji in Taoism.

I don't think it takes twenty years of meditating in a cave or monastery to develop the ability to experience dynamic stillness. However, some clear steps are needed. These steps focus on developing our connection to stillness, alongside developing sensory awareness, tuning in to nature and learning to allow and accept what we are experiencing. The final step is to observe our own thoughts, feelings and emotions. This means we learn to start accepting ourselves a little, which in turn can bring humility.

PRACTISING WITH AN EGO

If we practise this work with an ego, or a sense of ownership, we will not get very far; we will only go around in circles. This work cannot be owned. If we are lucky, we can catch a glimpse of the sheer wonder of life and its interconnectedness, an experience which is truly breathtaking. The practices themselves, though, require a developing humility and a deepening connection to nature and to each other. This humility and connection brings a respect for all life and maybe a wish to protect and preserve all life too.

CONNECTING DEEPLY TO OURSELVES, NATURE AND EACH OTHER

What is interesting is that this practice of dynamic stillness starts to change us. As we connect deeply to ourselves, nature, each other and the universe, our sense of responsibility changes. If we are all interconnected, we must care for and nurture one another, which is the most beautiful and natural thing in the universe. If we all learn to feel this interconnection, surely we will develop a deeper responsibility to the planet and each other?

The unusual feeling that we start to experience during this dynamic stillness practice is the sense of our body's edges dissolving, becoming transparent, so there is no boundary between us and the surrounding stillness. This feeling is new and wonderful.

PRACTICE 22

Dynamic Stillness

Begin the practice

For this practice you are going to try two very different methods to gain sensory awareness and experience of dynamic stillness.

1. Sitting with Heaven and Earth

Here, you are going to build on your previous technique of Connecting Heaven and Earth (*see pages 108–09*). This time you will adopt a sitting posture. Sit comfortably in whatever posture suits and feels comfortable. The lotus positions, especially the full lotus, were thought to be preferred in Hindu and Buddhist teachings. In the lotus posture, the palms and soles of the feet are facing up to the sky. I am still not flexible enough to do the lotus so I sit with a cushion under my bottom and this extra height makes it easier to cross my legs.

When you are comfortable in a chosen position, place your hands in your lap, palms facing upwards. Tune in to the softness of your breath and allow your body to come to neutral. This process should be quite easy by now.

You will repeat what you did in the Connecting Heaven and Earth technique.

To recap: as you breathe in, become aware of a light, delicate energy from above. The quality is like sunlight but slightly more. It resembles the subtle energy of the sun, stars and planets, or the universe as a whole. Breathe this energy into your lower stomach through every pore in your body, especially the top of your head and the palms of your hands.

As you repeat this technique five or six times, you should feel a soft, light energy fill and calm you. When you feel this quality, especially in your lower stomach, you are now ready to engage with the earth energy.

Turn your palms downwards and start by feeling the slightly stronger, deeper, vibrant quality of the earth. Widen your awareness to the earth around you and see if you can feel this quiet, deeply nurturing energy. As you breathe in, let the energy come through every pore, especially via your palms and the soles of your feet, into the lower stomach. Repeat for five to six breaths so you really get a sense of this nurturing earth energy in your body.

Rest your hands in your lap again in a neutral position. From here, you want to try to combine the above techniques. Split your awareness. On each in-breath, breathe in both heaven and earth energies from above and below. Relax as you breathe out. Repeat five or six times, relaxing more with each out-breath.

You may start to get a sense of developing stillness within the motion of breathing. It should begin to feel as though both energies you are breathing in are becoming one. Let this quality develop and the deep stillness – a dynamic stillness – build. You may get a sense that you are becoming light and full of this energy, which is the same both inside and outside of you, all around you and expands as far as the horizon. It is a deep and dynamic stillness that feels perfect, connected and profoundly peaceful.

After a few minutes, this sensation will naturally come to an end and you will start to feel a gentle fluidity, an inherent natural motion in your body, and your awareness of your surroundings will return. This is a natural end to the process.

2. The Stillness in the Tide

You may wish to try this technique immediately after the previous one, or you may find you want to come back to it next time you practise. If you get a nice experience of dynamic stillness, that is often enough.

For this practice, you are going to build on the technique for feeling the great tide, which you looked at in Chapter 13 (*see pages 70–1*). It is best to be sitting with a view of a horizon. As you get used to these techniques, though, you will find that you will have less need for visual access to landmarks and practices.

Sit comfortably and quietly, this time with your eyes closed, and allow your awareness to go slowly out, as if breathing it out towards the horizon. You don't need a direction, rather you need an overall awareness of a horizon. Instead of seeing the horizon, feel it with your developing felt-sense. Let your awareness just breathe out and meet the stillness that is already at the horizon. Can you feel it?

Once you have accessed this stillness, just wait with it and enjoy the feeling. After a little while, you will sense the tide slowly arise from the stillness on the horizon and slowly come towards you from one side. It isn't important where the tide comes from as this is a perceptual quality; sometimes it can approach from all sides. Let the tide breathe you – in other words, let it breathe through you, passing undiminished. The feeling is that you become connected to, or even become part of, this great tide.

Develop this concept a little more. As you feel the gentle movement of the tide, I want you to find somewhere in it – it could be the horizon, or a sensory quality within the motion – that is stillness. It is the stillness that is behind the tide.

Your perception will begin to shift as you start to feel a quality of total stillness, but a stillness that also has a great power in it, like a potential energy from which motion manifests. But it is more than motion: everything manifests from this dynamic stillness.

You can start to get a sense that you are a translucent, transparent part of this dynamic stillness. Quiet and yet powerful, this stillness has an almost sacred quality to it. Enjoy this quality for a little while – a few seconds, or a few minutes if you prefer – and be aware of its end point, which is very interesting. It feels as though you are reforming. The quality is one of wholeness, as though you are being re-created in that very moment.

CHAPTER 23

RETURNING TO THE NATURAL – TRUE CREATIVITY

One of our many purposes in this dynamic stillness work is to start to return to a natural response to life, where we are moved by the moment and begin to lose our conditioned responses to everyone and everything around us. In Taoism this has been termed 'the seat of spontaneity'.

True spontaneity has great potential for us. By its very nature it is deeply creative, meaning we start to create our lives moment by moment. This state of being is almost childlike. We begin to release historic, conditioned responses to life and start to act – as opposed to react – to life and its great ups and downs. This process starts with the simple step of learning to find a neutral state within ourselves. This neutrality proliferates as we develop a deepening connection to and understanding of the stillness within and around us. We learn to feel the great tide in nature and to experience dynamic stillness, which brings about the potential from which life creates itself moment to moment, as motion arises from stillness. As we experience and learn these processes, they can slowly change us. At the same time, we are looking at our senses and how they have been conditioned by our life experiences, a concept we will develop in the next chapters. Here, we will learn to release the conditioning of our senses in the hope of starting to experience life and the universe anew. As our rhythm connects and slows to the natural rhythms in nature, we start to feel our way through life, which brings a natural creativity and spontaneity.

TRUE CREATIVITY

What does it mean to be truly creative? Creative people tend to think for themselves and are often tasked with thinking ahead of the group. In indigenous tribes, such as the Bushmen of the Kalahari, the artists would produce beautiful cave paintings as it was their role to scribe, describe, document and inspire the other members of the tribe.

I am a great fan of art. Since they were young, my children have been dragged to galleries around the world and introduced to many great artworks. For me, the true artists inspired their own cultures and were at the cutting edge in the development of civilization. The great artists led the way in defining and understanding humans and their relationship to nature and the divine. This process may have been lost to some degree in recent generations but, in principle, the artist, the sculptor, the writer and the architect, for example, would spearhead the development of culture.

True artists have pure, spontaneous creativity. They engage with their surroundings and interpret them in ever-new ways, being instinctively moved to act in response to their senses. But I feel that every one of us can be the artist of our lives, no matter what we are doing. If we act spontaneously and creatively in response to our senses, we are being totally creative in each moment and our life can become an art form, a work of ever-changing art. It doesn't matter if we are painting pictures, painting the walls, caring for a baby or doing the washing-up – it is really not important. Once we are in rhythm with life and come from a true place of spontaneity, we become truly creative.

The process of 'returning to the natural' means we learn to consciously let go of conditioned responses to life. We become neutral to ourselves and, in doing so, we start to practise self-awareness and, most importantly, self-acceptance. With increased self-acceptance, something magical happens. As we allow, accept and observe, and finally become neutral to ourselves, we judge ourselves less and less. In doing so, we also start to judge others less and less, and learn to accept them. This acceptance brings with it a deeper sense of compassion and empathy.

Coming from 'the natural' includes greater self-acceptance. And in that greater acceptance for others that follows, there is a growing sense of neutral and connection to stillness, and dynamic stillness. With it, there is a deepening connection to nature and the tide, bringing a spontaneity and true creativity within each moment.

The unusual experience, when you enter a state of dynamic stillness, of feeling as though your body is dissolving into stillness and becoming transparent can act to make us more transparent. In that state, we are less affected by and have less effect on the nature around us. It is almost as though we become able to step with a lighter footprint.

PRACTICE 23

The Seat of Spontaneity

Begin the practice

For this practice, use the building blocks you have been using in each chapter thus far. Find a quiet place to sit for a while and enter a state of neutral by allowing, accepting and observing your thoughts, feelings and emotions – just let it all be.

Meet a deep sense of stillness

Now, let the outside presence of stillness penetrate, and as your mind settles, your presence increases.

Let your awareness breathe out to the horizon

With your eyes closed, use your felt-sense to feel the stillness on the horizon. Wait here for the tide to come in, to move from stillness to motion.

When you get a solid sense of the tide, follow it, returning to the horizon and going again to the sense of stillness from which it comes. This can bring a feeling of a deeper stillness with a power – you can sense a softening of your body's 'edges' and a dynamic stillness, power and potential within stillness.

Bring your attention back to yourself

See yourself, connected to the tide and, through it, to the underlying dynamic stillness within the universe or multiverse.

Fulcrum point

Wait at this fulcrum point from which the dynamic stillness is pregnant with expression, wanting to create the manifest from the unmanifest. Try to feel out how the universe is creating this moment for you and what you need to do right now. Try to use this dynamic within the stillness to guide a deep, instinctual part of yourself.

Conclusion

Again, this process is all about developing a stronger sense of connection. Allow yourself to be moved by the moment, freely and fluidly. It feels as though you are being held by life, safe and aware. Like sitting in the seat of spontaneity, you are totally free to be moved by the moment.

$\mathscr{S}$TILLNESS $\mathscr{P}$ROLIFERATES

As our practice develops and deepens, there are a number of positive processes that occur. It is like planting seeds in well-tended, watered soil with the right conditions of sunlight and weather, which we are starting to create through our practices. But what is growing within us is more than the practice. It is the beautiful flower that we planted as a seed, or the wonderful fruit that we never expected would grow.

We start to become more accepting and more neutral to ourselves, practising more self-love and self-care. An interesting side effect of greater self-love is that we naturally become more accepting of others. We also develop a deepening relationship to the great natural stillness that is all around us. We tune in our senses to this natural stillness so we can feel it at will and it can start to enter our consciousness spontaneously. We also deepen our relationship with our internal stillness, which starts to enter our everyday life and the people around us can enjoy an increased feeling of peace when they are near us. Connecting with the tide slows our natural rhythms. Feeling calm, we start to feel a deeper connection with nature.

By aligning ourselves to dynamic stillness, we can start to feel truly spontaneous, moved by the moment, and almost as if we are linked to the universe. Through these combined processes our practice deepens. If we bring our awareness to this process of proliferation, it grows even more.

PRACTICE 24

Stillness Proliferates

Begin the practice

For this practice, start in the same manner as always, but once you start to feel stillness in or around you, or the tide or dynamic stillness, stop doing anything.

Watch the stillness proliferate

Sit, relax and watch as stillness proliferates naturally. You aren't bringing your aware-ness to anything; you are sitting, allowing your awareness to be breathed by the moment, with no technique. You are simply enjoying this deepening process.

Conclusion

Try to sense this naturally spontaneous, proliferating stillness and how it develops. Take a moment to ask yourself, 'What is deepening it?' If we wait with our attention lightly on this stillness, it seems to proliferate.

CHAPTER 25

MEETING OUR HEALTH

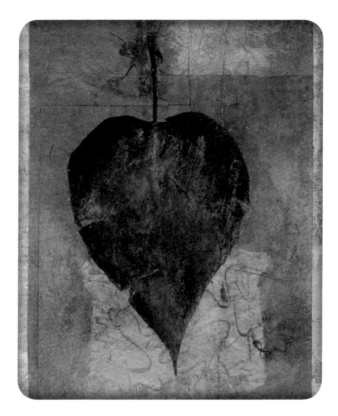

As we start to feel a deepening connection to natural rhythms outside in nature and inside our body, and as we deepen our relationship to stillness and dynamic stillness, a natural progression is to start to orientate ourselves to our capacity for health.

The World Health Organization defines health as a level of functional and metabolic efficiency of a living organism. It goes on to say that 'Health is a state of complete physical, mental and social wellbeing and not merely the absence of disease or infirmity'. This definition has prevailed since 1948, though it is seen as controversial mainly due to its abstract nature.

SELF-AWARENESS AND THE SENSES

For our practice, what we are interested in is exploring our own relationship with health. What does 'health' mean for you? A healthy body, a healthy mind, to love and be loved? A healthy relationship with ourselves and others, with our community? With our children? Our parents? With our significant other? Can we be healthy if our body is not quite right?

Health, for me, is a perception. It is a perception of self that develops very early on in our lives. It relates to the idea of consciousness – by which I mean self-awareness of one's own existence, sensations, thoughts, feelings, individually or collectively.

Sensations come from internal sense organs and our five senses, which interpret the outer world. These senses are then filtered through the higher centres of our brain, combining with our emotional state and our thoughts and beliefs. The result of all this activity combines to give us a sense of consciousness – awareness of self and our surroundings.

There is one more sense that we have already mentioned: the felt-sense, which uses a combination of our senses and internal awareness to sense stillness, tides and fluidity. As we work to become neutral, we are trying to unlock this felt-sense from our thoughts, beliefs, emotions and feelings.

LEARNING TO FEEL OUR HEALTH

An important part of this journey is to start to learn to feel our health. Health is more than a concept, it is something that can be felt within our body. What's more, if we learn to tune in to this health, we can harness it to heal ourselves and, eventually, to heal others.

Health has a sensory quality, a felt-sense that feels like a gentle, fluid, light expression that is present within the body. There is an inherent freedom in the expression, a motion or a freedom to move. This can be felt in the whole body, or a specific isolated area. There are certain prerequisites for us to acquire to be able to feel this aliveness, this expression of health in our body, which we have learnt on this journey.

Let's look again at how our senses, both internal and external, are patterned from early on, before we are born. My feeling is that we are attuned early in life to what hurts, what feels blocked and what doesn't feel nice. There is an important reason for this orientation to pain and blockage: self-preservation.

Pain is an interesting phenomenon. What is pain? It is our brain's interpretation of stimulation of certain receptors in the body.

ALTERING OUR PERCEPTION OF OUR HEALTH

Pain is not a fixed perception, which means we can alter our response to it. There are gates at various levels of the brain, which allow input from cognitive, emotional or other senses and can increase or decrease the sensation of pain. For example, you can elicit a soothing response from a baby by putting them to their mother's breast after a painful injection. This act to modifies the response of the body to pain. All our senses, whether internal or external, are open to being modulated by our feelings, thoughts, emotions and beliefs.

What is important to take from this is that our understanding of health is complex. It comes from sensory experience and emotional makeup, both of which were wired into our brains early on. Even more significant, in my view, is that our thoughts, feelings and perceptions of our health can be remodelled and reshaped into something that is better for us. We need our internal and external sensory awareness to ascertain if there is danger in our environment. For example, we move our hand away from a hot stove. Or, in our primitive history, we learnt to fight or run from a wild animal.

FOCUSING ON WHAT FEELS 'GOOD' NOT 'WRONG'

Focusing on problems with our health has diverted us away from gaining a good relationship with what feels good and healthy in our body, which we *do* know how to feel. Our nervous systems have a deep memory of the comfort of our mother's touch, smell and voice. Our senses can be soothed by beauty, by wonderful-tasting foods and human touch. But rarely are we focused on that abstract sense of health, of feeling the potential for wellbeing within our body.

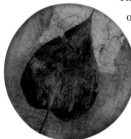

This lack of focus on the health in our body is compounded by overwhelming external noise, the ever quickening pace of life and by constant sensory overload. Where is there time and space to feel this delicate expression of health in our body? It is, however, vital that we find the time to do so. There is an old adage that says, 'What you focus on grows'. This, I think, is true.

We have learnt since we were very young to focus on what feels 'wrong' in our bodies and so, to learn to self-heal, we must repattern our brain not to feel what is wrong, but to feel what is right, what feels healthy, fluid and even light in the body.

LEARNING TO SELF-HEAL

To refocus on health and to learn to self-heal, we must go through a series of steps we have been building on with each chapter. Here, we are trying to repattern, or rewire, our brains, like creating a new path to walk on. This process takes repeated work and practice.

Now, we need those three tenets of accepting, allowing and observing our thoughts, feelings, emotions and even our beliefs. We must deepen our relationship to stillness, dynamic stillness and the tide. From here, we can start to re-orientate our senses – internal, external and the felt-sense – to health.

Meeting the Health

Begin your practice

Sit comfortably, bringing your attention and awareness to the stillness around you. Wait for that stillness to calm you to neutral.

By now, your body is repatterning, knowing the path to follow, and deepening its connection to stillness.

Bring your awareness to a specific point

With your palms facing down, bring your awareness to a patch of skin on the back of your hands. Sense the weight of the air on the skin. Can you feel it? This is bringing your sensory awareness specifically to one spot and sensing something that you usually tune out (if you do not tune out most sensory impressions, there would be too many).

Bring your awareness to the skin all over your body. Can you feel the air on it all? It doesn't matter if you feel it through your clothes, you can still feel it.

Shift your awareness to the your body

How does your body feel? Can you name that feeling? Are you tired? What does 'tired' feel like? Does your body feel uncomfortable? In what way? Can you name it?

Allow your awareness to meet a location that feels fluid

Now, switch your perception. Is there anywhere in your body that feels nice, that feels fluid, delicate, light or free to move? Allow your awareness to meet any location in your body that feels nice and let your attention rest there. What happens? Does that fluid feeling expand?

Conclusion

Bring your awareness to your skin again. Feel the weight of the air on it. Now soften your awareness, allow your skin, your edges, to soften, to become more fluid, and breathe. This usually starts in one place, then other areas catch up until everything feels soft and fluid around your edges. Enjoy that quality for a few minutes and bring your awareness to what is around you, then sense when you feel the tide coming.

$\mathscr{S}$ELF-HEALING

Is it possible to heal oneself? Can we have any influence at all on the balance and healthiness of our body? We often have the perception that our body systems 'do their thing' without our interference, but we do have an influence on the potential for health within our body.

Everything we ingest can be harmful or helpful to our body. Toxicity in the environment can have a significant effect on our health and wellbeing. Even our emotions can influence our body. Stress – or distress – has been shown to agitate certain elements of our nervous system, with a knock-on effect on our immune system. Our health, then, seems to be a complex combination of the natural balance within our body and its response to the environment we inhabit, along with emotional, nutritional and potential toxic elements, and our genetic makeup.

How closely connected is our perception of health to our actual health? In my osteopathy practice I meet very healthy people whose perception of their health is poor, because of whatever beliefs they hold and their emotional state, which has a strong effect on health perception. On the other hand, I often meet people who are quite unwell, with cancer or states of chronic disease, but who have positive perceptions of their health. They often seem more attuned to the potential for their health than the underlying disease state.

OUR INNER HEALING PROCESSES

We see that health, to a large degree, comes down to our perception of it. I would argue that the first step in the process of self-healing is to alter our perception of health – to change our underlying view of how we perceive our body from one of looking at the problems, the lesions, to looking at the potential health that is always there, even if we are quite ill.

I outlined in the previous chapter that this change in perception is the first stage, but how can we move on and attempt to start to heal ourselves? Is it even possible to influence our internal physiology? I would argue that we could change these internal states to varying degrees, depending on the underlying potential for health. If we learn to focus on and pay attention to the inner natural healing processes within our body, the act of paying attention increases the potency and effect of these processes.

The act of focusing is a basic principle of treating a patient with osteopathy. We treat patients with a wide variety of issues by learning to find the potential for health within the body and supporting that internal process. If it is applied very precisely, this simple idea can be profound.

HOMEOSTASIS

Each of us has an incredible potential to heal and restore function in areas that are not functioning properly. We do so every second of our lives. It is called homeostasis, the process of maintaining an internal steady state, or a state of physiological equilibrium. This balance happens constantly within our bodies, from the simplest to the most complex ways. For example, our body metabolizes its food needs, creating energy and waste products, which are then processed by the body. If we train hard and strain a muscle group, it repairs itself very quickly unless the strain is too severe. If we break a bone, it usually heals in days to weeks. The body is incredible at this process of healing itself.

A BETTER EXPRESSION OF HEALTH

Disease often occurs if these self-healing mechanisms fail us; if the strain is too much, if the break is too bad or the natural chemistry of the body stops functioning correctly, a state of disease ensues. But can we affect this? Can we enhance our body's ability to heal? I would argue that we can; I would also argue that we can heal others.

In order for the techniques of self-healing to be effective, we need to set up certain preconditions. If we don't do this, self-healing become very hard to achieve. But, as with all these techniques, practice makes perfect. First, we become neutral to ourselves and learn to allow our attention to gently stay with these tiny, delicate forces as they act within our body – these fluid, light potencies acting to restore function and balance. The trick here is that what we focus on grows, so by giving precise attention to these forces, a magic thing seems to happen. These forces strengthen, which gives a wonderful, warm, healing sense to the tissue we are focusing on. If we repeat this a few times, the body can start to engage with it quite easily and the hope is that these growing forces can help the body find a better expression of health or balance.

I would argue that if we focus our awareness correctly, this technique can be helpful when conditions are severe and when dealing with acute and chronic pain, even if it is extreme. However, with severe pain such as bone pain from secondary cancer or the neurological pain of Trigeminal neuralgia (chronic pain disorder), it takes a massive effort of will for the sufferer not to become overwhelmed by it. I have taught these techniques to people with both these conditions, which inflict some of the worst pains imaginable. In both cases, these patients reported some lessening of pain.

Whatever the situation, from experiencing severe metastatic (tumour-related) pain to feeling a little under the weather, to having a minor ache in your little finger or just wanting to support your body's health, the technique remains the same. We can apply the same practice to emotional states, too. If we are feeling weighed down by grief, sadness or depression, we can use the self-healing practice on the following pages to soften the feelings and make them more manageable.

PRACTICE 26

Self-healing

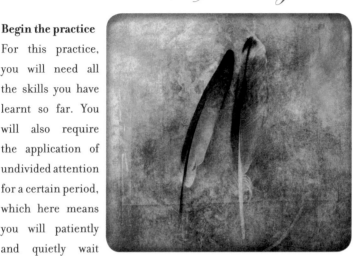

Begin the practice

For this practice, you will need all the skills you have learnt so far. You will also require the application of undivided attention for a certain period, which here means you will patiently and quietly wait with your attention on this potential health, this aliveness. It will take a bit of time to get used to this technique but each time you attemp it, it will get easier.

Begin by sitting or by lying down comfortably. Tune in to something that feels soft, fluid and delicate within your breathing. From here, allow and accept all the thoughts, feelings and emotions that arise. Observe them arising and falling away for a few minutes.

Bring awareness to the stillness within

Now, try to sense a quality of stillness within your body. Start to bring your awareness to some part of you that feels fluid well, and healthful, even light in its quality. It could be the tiniest micro-spot of fluidity. Allow this sense of fluidity within you to breathe and to expand naturally, by bringing your awareness to it.

Wait with this part of the practice for a few minutes until you start to get a sense of fluidity in your whole body, almost as though it becomes one drop of water. If this doesn't happen, don't worry, just keep your awareness on something that feels sweet and fluid.

Focus on an area that feels blocked

Change your attention to sense somewhere in your body that feels blocked, dark and non-fluid. Just focus on it lightly.

Focus on that light awareness of your blocked area. Within the block there is the tiniest speck of light and fluidity. Sometimes it feels like the memory of light, fluid potency, just a tiny spot within the block. It is always there. Sometimes you must wait, with the knowledge and trust that it *is* there. When you see that fluidity, completely focus your attention on it. Forget the rest of the block and keep your attention on the light, fluid potential.

Keep your awareness on the light

Something amazing happens here. The light, fluid area starts to grow and in doing so, starts to change the surrounding block, softening and lightening it. Keep your awareness on the light, fluid speck as it grows and starts to meet the general fluidity in the body.

As the block softens and lightens, the fluids in the body become quiet and still. At that moment, open your awareness to the stillness around you. You may then be able to feel the tide come in.

The end point of this moment is when everything returns to a gentle fluidity. The block may not have gone completely, but it will feel somewhat better.

Conclusion

The principle is the same with pain and with difficult emotions. Just go through the same steps and stay with the potential for lightness and fluidity, even within the darkest feeling. Sometimes you must just trust in the potential for the lightness to come, even if you cannot see it at first. If you get stuck, simply go back to allowing whatever thoughts, feelings or emotions want to come up, accept and then observe them. Then bring your attention back to the potential for an expression of health. This expression is always there; it is just hidden sometimes, especially if the pain is severe.

At the beginning, try this practice once or twice. It will start to get easier the more often you do it and then something important happens: you begin to change your focus onto your health, rather than any pain. The effect of this can be profound.

CHAPTER 27

*M*EETING THE *H*EALTH IN *O*THERS

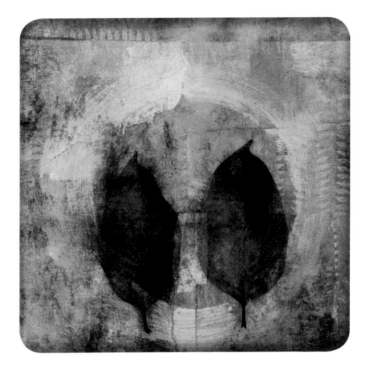

In the previous two chapters we started to change our way of looking at ourselves. We have moved away from seeing our own blocks, deficits and lesions, whether physical, emotional or spiritual. From there, we have felt what health is like in ourselves and developed a practice on the process of self-healing. It is important for us to gain an experience of, and a developing relationship with, these principles before we go on to apply them to others. Others, in this case, being friends, family, acquaintances, but also nature itself. We can learn to apply these principles for treating pets, or even suffering plants.

HOW WE THINK OF OTHERS

What we must start with is, once again, a fundamental change in perspective, followed by a developing sensory experience of what health feels like in another person. To meet the health in others, we must first be open to the idea of it. Just as with our view of ourselves, we are usually all too aware of the faults in others, even our loved ones. Often we focus our attention on what irritates us about those around us, alongside our feelings of love for them. For this stage in our practice, we must become conscious of our own thinking about others and make any necessary changes to this. What I am saying here is that, for these purposes, we must actively choose to see something quite lovely, perfect and beautiful about the person or living thing that we are choosing to focus on. I am not saying that we ignore the difficult aspects, but rather that we bring our attention directly onto something that is sweet, delicate and fluid in them. This is before we even touch them. The sense comes first from our mental viewpoint. It is an interesting exercise to do, and we will play with this idea in the practice that follows this chapter.

To meet the health of another person, we must first shift our perspective, where we mentally place our attention onto something that we like in the person. It could be anything about them. But we meet, or engage with them through something that is nice, delicate or beautiful in them. It is much harder to try to see something lovely – even just the tiniest idea of something that is sweet or even likable – about someone or something that we find repugnant. But it is quite freeing to do, even if we can only do it for the tiniest moment. This process is similar to dynamic stillness, which we covered in Chapter 22 (*see pages 112–17*). It provides an inroad to meeting the person in the correct manner, vital in the process of healing. If we are going to try to engage a healing process in another person, we must first start with this more positive way of thinking. It is absolutely vital.

LOVING KINDNESS

This process brings to mind a Tibetan Buddhist practice called 'Loving Kindness', in which one chants or says to oneself the following:

'May I be happy, may I be well.'

Then, after repeating this a few times, we bring our attention to another person. First, think of a loved one and then say:

'May you be happy, may you be well.'

From here, we bring our attention to someone who we know but neither like nor dislike (the bank teller, someone you see on the bus) and say:

'May they be happy, may they be well.'

Now we can bring our attention to someone we really dislike. They may have been harmful to us or others, and say:

'May they be happy, may they be well.'

The clever part of this practice is that it refocuses our attention on the health of others and ourselves. On a subtler level, it works to bring a degree of self-acceptance to elements within ourselves that we are not happy with.

If the outer world is just a reflection of our inner world, accepting and wishing well to other people we do not like must reflect a level of self-love. This is a very healing practice and one we should try for a few minutes every day. There is something in this practice that is liberating and beautiful.

For our purposes, then, we must first select the person or thing we wish to engage with. This is much easier to do with someone or something we love because it is easy to meet their health. We can graduate to healing others who we are not naturally moved to love at a later stage. It doesn't matter what element of this person we focus on. We could turn our attention to their hair, to their outfit, to the way they smile or to the love they show. Just focus on one element of the person that is sweet and allow the feeling of love to develop for that element. What I am asking us to do here, really, is to feel what it is like, to enjoy something about another person.

PRACTICE 27

Meeting the Health in Others

Begin the practice

Use your feelings and your imagination — that is enough for your purposes now.

Think about someone you love

Close your eyes and feel what it is like to love them. Is it a warm glow in your chest, or is it an overwhelmingly strong feeling? It doesn't matter what the feeling is, just allow yourself to feel it.

Bring your attention to what you love about this person

Is it their smile, the way they talk to you, their generosity or their inner beauty? Whatever it is, allow yourself to respond to how that makes you feel. Remember that feeling — you are going to come back to it later.

Bring your attention to someone you barely know

It helps if you can remember them a little. Focus your awareness on something about them that you like, whether it is their coat, their hair or the way they gave up their seat on the crowded bus. Focus what it feels like, with your awareness.

Bring your attention to someone you do not like

Can you imagine one thing about them that is nice — a gesture, a word? If you find it difficult, imagine them as a child smiling at their mother, or another simple human quality that you do not usually see. Again, try to feel this quality, this meeting of the part of them that is health.

Bring your attention to an animal or plant

Tune in to something you love about the animal or plant and allow yourself to focus on how that makes you feel.

Practice the 'loving kindness' technique

Start with yourself: 'May I be happy, may I be well.' Then repeat the process for, first, a loved one, then someone you barely know and, finally, someone who really annoys you:

'May you be happy, may you be well.'

'May they be happy, may they be well.'

CHAPTER 28

Wholeness Meeting Oneness

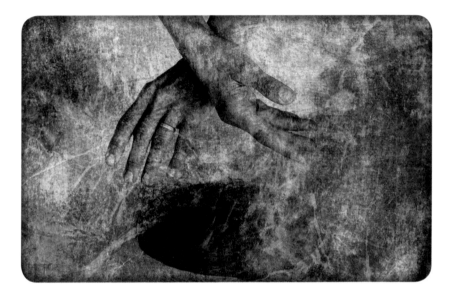

There is an underlying process that quietly proliferates as we continue to develop our practice. As we connect more with our own fluid body, as we become more neutral to ourselves, as we get a felt-sense of the stillness that is all around us and within us and as we develop a deeper connection to the tide, something starts to happen to us. When we feel our fluid body as a single drop, breathing and in connection with an outer stillness or the gentle motion of the tide, we start to feel a sense of wholeness.

Wholeness is defined in the Oxford English Dictionary as 'the state of forming a complete and harmonious whole, a unity'. This is what we can start to feel within us as we practise more and more. We give birth to a state of self-acceptance that harmonizes us. We acquire a sense of wholeness, as though we are complete, which brings with it a growing feeling of peace and harmony.

We become attuned to a sense of fluidity in our bodies, vital healthfulness and wellbeing, and start to enjoy this strengthening connection to nature and ourselves as our perception of how our body feels begins to shift.

WHAT IT MEANS TO FEEL WHOLE

What does it mean to feel whole? For me, it involves a deep sense of self-acceptance. We may not be perfect or a hundred per cent healthy, but we accept all the different parts of us. Our self-judgement softens as the fluidity we are feeling increases.

In the process of self-acceptance, something else happens. We start to accept and feel a deepening connection with others and the natural world around us. We get a palpable experience of the stillness and the tide that connects us all, and through that connection we feel part of a united whole. We feel a 'oneness' – a profound link – with that wider or greater whole, and a natural consequence of this is to start to feel part of nature and part of others. With this inevitably comes a deepening respect for other people and all of nature around us, and a sense of responsibility for it.

For me, this is one of the most important side effects of engaging in a health-giving practice. Through this deepening connection – and, hence, respect and responsibility – it becomes harder to be blind to the effect we have on our surroundings. I hope this means that we walk more softly on the earth, that we do not disturb it and that we become more accountable for the nature around us.

Through our practice, we can begin to heal ourselves and others, and even support the nature around us. From our developing sensory awareness, we start to sense things we never thought possible and take notice of the detail in nature we have missed in the past. We slow our innate tempo to one that is more instinctively in sync with nature, which reinforces the connection with it and deepens the feeling of oneness.

As you see, we are not just thinking thoughts of wholeness and oneness, we are feeling them. This brings them alive and makes them real to us. It goes beyond a simple concept and gives us a sense of experience. It takes us from a belief into a reality that we can experience at will.

Wholeness Meets Oneness

Begin the practice

Start by sitting in comfort and tuning in to your breathing, and then accepting, allowing, observing everything that arises in the moment.

**Bring your awareness
to the stillness**

As everything quietens down, bring your awareness to the underlying stillness behind all noise and motion. All motion begins as stillness, just as all life begins in stillness, as everything manifest starts in the unmanifest. Feel this stillness and let it build.

Bring your attention to your body

Sense something that feels fluid. No matter how small, follow the fluid, the delicate expression of fluid health within your body. Let this fluidity expand and open so that a bigger and bigger area of your body starts to feel fluid.

Now expand your light attention to your whole body. It is like opening your vision to a wider view.

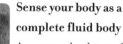

**Sense your body as a
complete fluid body**

As you slowly and gently breathe, integrate the parts of your body and connect them up, softening, calming and becoming one. Continue as your body starts to feel like a single fluid drop with no boundary, no anatomy, just a single fluid drop, breathing slowly with primary respiration.

Conclusion

Bring your attention to the horizon now and get a sense of the stillness that lies there. Get a sense of the stillness that is everywhere, holding and connecting us all. You are one drop within a sea, all calm and quiet. From the quiet comes the slow great tide, breathing you and then returning to the stillness so very slowly; your wholeness meeting a greater wholeness, becoming a oneness.

CHAPTER 29

REPATTERNING OUR SENSES: DEVELOPING A FELT-SENSE

As I talked about in Chapter 14 (*see pages 72–7*), our five senses develop quite early in utero. Our senses of smell, touch and hearing are fairly well formed by thirty weeks' gestation. From this stage onwards, we are patterning our senses by creating connections between sensations, emotions and feelings. For example, the first things we hear are the muffled sounds of our mother's voice and heartbeat. These sound rhythms connect us deeply with a sense of nurture and support.

Our early sense of touch is formed by touching our own face and body and is also developed by contact with our mother and the feeling of being held in a warm, protective sea of amniotic fluid. We are naked within this sea, so the touch sensors in our whole body become used to this nurturing, warm fluid as it holds us safely.

With taste and smell, once again the first thing we sense is our mother, through the amniotic fluid, breast milk and her unique smell. These imbue, as before, a deep sense of connection and nurture.

From birth onwards, we are bombarded through our senses. A newborn sees without precision, but the brain quickly wires up and can see very accurately from just six months of age. Our senses are designed from the beginning to detect simple elements that we need for basic survival. In simple terms, they connect us with the external environment. We need to detect the basic idea of whether there is threat or nurture in the surrounding environment and we can then respond reflexively to either.

The way the nervous system has been shown to develop is that once the basic instincts for survival are dealt with, such as threat or nurture, we can then go on to develop our social brain. Our social brain enables us to communicate and show emotion, through smiling and other social gestures.

SENSORY AWARENESS

The importance of our senses in this developing story of our nervous system plays a meaningful but subtle role in the way we use our senses as adults. From early on, we are inundated by myriad sense impressions. We quickly learn to screen out non-vital inputs.

As we develop consciousness, our thinking brain – the front of the brain, including the frontal lobes and the emotion-regulating limbic parts of the brain – applies a certain discernment in the way that we apply our senses. But the early experiences that have shaped us leave a silent imprint and preconsciously guide our attention. As we grow and develop, it is only what we put our attention onto that we sense, and we screen out most of the elements taken in by our senses. This sensory awareness also gets shaped early on by the structure of the brain and the proximity of each sense to different parts of the brain.

Our visual and hearing centres are much closer to the language part of the brain, so we find it much easier to describe sounds and visual stimuli. As we grow, we build up a complex, highly discerning sensory memory.

CATEGORIZING OUR SENSORY EXPERIENCES

We categorize each distinct sensory experience we have in many conscious and unconscious ways. Unconsciously, we are always distinguishing between threats and nurture. Other instinctual drives – such as sexual attraction – complicate the process.

Each thing that we see, hear, smell, taste or touch goes through multiple layers of screening. Most of them are discarded by preconscious parts of the brain so they are not even registered. It takes quite a lot of stimuli to provoke a conscious reaction to something that we sense.

An important question for us here is: are our five senses all we use to sense the world around us or is there more to it? Each cell in our body has its own skin, called its membrane. The cell membrane is highly sensory. It is sensitive and reactive to the environment around it and it reacts within the cell to alter its function and even switch genes on and off. These receptors are influenced by many things in the surrounding environment, from subtle fluid changes, to electromagnetic changes to biochemical changes. You could say that each cell in our body has a sensory awareness. If you think of the billions of cells we are made up of and how they function together, we can start to see that our whole body is a sensory apparatus. We are totally sensory!

Consider the growing science behind the idea that our heart acts as more than just a pump. We all have an inkling that our hearts have a greater role, especially when it comes to our emotions. We have all felt heartache; it is a real sense coming from our chest and it is emotional. There is increasing evidence that is corroborated by our own sensory experience that our heart is also a sensory organ – in that we can feel and connect through our heart with the world and with other people. When we consider all of this together, we must come to regard our senses as many more than our five sensory organs.

We started to explore these themes in earlier chapters, but here we want to really develop our sensory experience so that we are far more conscious of its full potential. The idea of a felt-sense expands our usual view of our senses. This sense is not made up of any particular sense but includes an ever-changing combination of senses. Using it we can learn to sense throughout the entirety of our system, as though we are one huge cell membrane that can sense the environment on multiple levels at the same time.

MULTI-LEVEL SENSORY AWARENESS

This idea of a multi-level sensory awareness is very much facilitated by the feeling of fluidity. If we sense the world through our fluid body, we become totally sensory. All our individual senses connect to allow us to have overall impressions, which are felt within a fluid field. It is as if we are a fluid field, which is purely sensory, engaging with the world around, which is also fluid and sensory. Maybe this is due to our earliest sensing of the world being entirely fluid within the amniotic-fluid-filled womb.

If we can become skilled at engaging with the world via this fluid field, the result can be that our senses begin to renew, refresh and repattern, lose their learnt biases and become open to sensing the beauty of the world around us. We literally start to sense the world around us differently.

PRACTICE 29

Felt-sense

Felt-sense is the opposite to a thinking, analytical way of seeing the world. It is about sensing without judgement and being open to experience the world through your developing sensory awareness. For this practice your mind must be neutral so you minimize any mental projections of what you are sensing.

Begin the practice

Start by sitting quietly and sensing a degree of stillness behind everything. You are sensing this underlying stillness with what I call the felt-sense. You cannot hear or see the stillness, but you can feel it. This sensory apparatus employs all your senses: it is more than any sense by itself and more than all five senses combined.

Attune to your fluid body

Sense a degree of fluidity somewhere within your body and allow, accept and observe any thoughts, feelings and emotions that then arise. Once you find some fluidity, allow this to expand. Slowly, you will feel yourself becoming fluid, a fluid body slowly breathing, which can then be used to sense your surroundings.

Keep an awareness of your fluid body as you sense the stillness all around you and let that perception deepen naturally.

Allow your felt-sense to breathe

As before, allow your felt-sense to breathe out to the horizon and wait until you feel the great tide – a motion coming from stillness, holding you and connecting you to life.

Allow your felt-sense to expand and try to sense something in your environment, be it a plant, flower or person. Do not touch it, but allow this felt-sense from your fluidity to meet and sense the fluidity of the chosen person or thing. Can you feel it? Without using touch in the usual way, we can start to feel or sense our surroundings.

Conclusion

This is your felt-sense and it will connect you to yourself and to nature, bringing a sense of oneness to everything. It will also expand and deepen your sensory experience.

CHAPTER 30

SENSING WHOLENESS IN NATURE

When the French philosopher René Descartes stated, 'I think therefore I am,' he introduced the concept of dualism, meaning that the process of thinking is key to our understanding of the world. Through this Cartesian approach, we see nature as separate to ourselves. The subject (us) and the object (nature) become two separate entities, and through the process of thought, we learn to understand nature.

A materialistic approach to science has been borne out of this dualistic concept. Science has sought to understand nature by quantifying and measuring it. This process of anyalysis breaks down nature into its components, then tries to put these elements together to understand the whole. Unfortunately, this concept is compounded by the idea that there are many ways of seeing the same thing. For example, the idea that the Earth is flat, stationary and at the centre of the universe makes a good deal of sense if we use our senses in a normal way. How could the Earth be moving through space at a great speed and still feel stable? The Polish astronomer Nicolaus Copernicus turned the world upside down by stating that the Earth and all the planets move around the sun. He had no evidence of this at the time, but he employed a jump in understanding in stating that 'if the Earth is moving, we in fact will be moving with it so would not feel the motion'.

In many ways, science has not, until recently, thought past this Cartesian dualistic approach. But one person who did was Johann Wolfgang von Goethe. Goethe was principally known as a poet and philosopher, based in Germany. During a trip to Italy in 1788, he became fascinated with the wealth of flowers and plants he saw in the countryside there, and with Renaissance painting. Subsequently, he spent twenty years researching colours, optics and the biology of plants.

Goethe started to see nature from a different perspective. He looked at the inherent wholeness of nature and perceived the whole deeply. He also developed the idea that to observe nature deeply, one becomes a participant in the process. This truly holistic approach removes the dualistic Cartesian concept of a subject being separate from an object: it reconnects them. Goethe looked deeply at the flowering plants and perceived that the plant was not made up of constituent parts but of a wholeness that becomes each part.

This idea can be thought of in terms of a hologram. A hologram is a photographic plate produced by a particularly sharp laser, which holds light together without it dispersing. If we take a pixel of a normal photograph or picture, we see just one part of the whole, but what is amazing about a hologram is that each pixel contains an image of the whole. In a normal picture, if we take away some of its parts, we will lose the coherence of the picture. If we remove some parts of the hologram, however, we retain the image but just a little bit more dispersed. The hologram is a nice example of wholeness because each part contains the whole.

Goethe expanded this thinking to the idea of morphology, a term he coined for the study of the inherent shapes in plants and animals. He would sense a plant or animal, looking deeply into its nature. This is an interesting idea to try out practically. As soon as we attempt to apply rational, analytic language, we are using a different part of our brain. We quickly lose the inherent ability to sense this wholeness and oneness. For example, while listening to birdsong this morning, my partner said, 'I wish that I could understand what they are saying.' I encouraged her to try a little 'holistic listening', asking her to employ her felt-sense at the same time. The process went as follows:

We started to sense the birdsong as a whole. This involved softening our hearing to detect the many birds that were singing as one holistic entity. 'But what am I supposed to hear?' she asked. My response was that there is no 'supposed to' about it. If we suppose anything, we are bringing in our analytic mind. 'Let's feel the birdsong as a whole, as a unity within which are all the different birds,' I answered. This was easier to understand and soon we could both feel the birdsong as a whole. Then I asked her, 'Try to feel, not hear, what they are saying within the wholeness. Do not employ language or try to apply a language to what you feel or hear.' This was possible and, without putting words to it, we could sense what the birds were saying but not within our human language.

Approaching the birdsong in this way brought us into a deep sense of connection with the birds and the birdsong. The idea that observer and observed become part of the phenomenon being observed is something that we start to sense. This may sound strange, but we will try it in the practice that follows this chapter and I hope you will get a sensory impression of it.

Throughout history there have been stories of Taoist wizards, shamans or healers from many indigenous cultures, who learnt to connect their energy with that of certain elements in nature. They used their connection with nature to heal others. The process seemingly involved a sharpened and expanded sensory awareness and even changed weather patterns.

This idea of holistic felt-sense can open up a whole new way of engaging with the world. By learning to sense nature holistically, we can deepen our connection and gain some amazing insights from it. This can make us holistic scientists of nature, by sensing natural processes deeply to gain a richer understanding of ourselves, and nature.

It is interesting that the scientific works of Goethe were discounted at the time, when Newtonian analytical views of science were preferred. Recently, especially through some of the findings from modern physics – including the idea that the observer has a measurable effect on the observed – this thinking has started to change.

Since the 1960s, science has understood more about the idea that a scientific viewpoint will vary due to there being different ways of seeing the same phenomena and the scientific philosophy of Goethe has begun to be reviewed. More interest has been shown in the idea of looking at phenomena in nature holistically, deeply observing it as a whole – not as a way of replacing analytic science, but as another method of looking into nature in which to better understand it.

The English poet and painter William Blake lived at the same time as Goethe. I do not know if they knew each other's work, but I see a great affinity between the two. In his poem 'Auguries of Innocence', written in 1803, Blake says:

> *To see a world in a grain of sand,*
> *And a heaven in a wild flower,*
> *Hold infinity in the palm of your hand,*
> *And eternity in an hour.*

These words, for me, echo the act of observing wholeness that Goethe employed and explain it beautifully. They hold a deep meaning and open up to us a wealth of possibilities when we allow ourselves to sense the world deeply and in wholeness.

Holistic Felt-sense

At this stage, you should be familiar with, and becoming proficient at, a variety of practices. You can bring your mind to a quiet neutral, where you allow, accept and finally observe your thoughts, feelings and emotions. You can bring your awareness to the present moment, feel your fluid body and sense stillness in and around you. From the stillness, you can sense the motion of the great tide as it slowly breathes through nature. You have started to develop your sensory awareness and to repattern your senses, and in so doing, have begun to develop a felt-sense through which you can expand your sensory awareness to feel nature around you.

Begin the practice

For this practice, you will take things a little further away from your analytic mind, to your open sensory field of awareness. In doing so, you will open yourself to new and beautiful impressions of nature.

Start with sitting quietly outside in nature. It doesn't matter if it is night-time or daytime.

Bring your mind to a quiet neutral

As you have done many times, now bring your mind to a quiet neutral, bringing your attention slowly back to the softness in your breath. Allow your attention to rest on the great stillness that is everywhere and behind everything.

Choose something in nature to observe

It doesn't matter what you observe and it is not important what primary sense you use. You could, for example, listen to birdsong, look at a flower or feel wind on your cheek. Below is the birdsong example.

Listen to the song, then try to listen to all the birds singing together. Allow your mind to sense them all as a unified whole, which is 'birdsong'. From here, let your felt-sense meet this wholeness of birdsong and try to feel it. Feeling the wholeness has the wonderful effect of connecting you deeply to the birdsong, doesn't it? It is almost as if you become part of the unified birdsong.

There are two elements to this sensing. The first is depth – you are sensing deeply,

as if penetrating the superficial to sense a deeper story within the whole. The second element is breadth – taking in the whole. This is not an overview but an opening of our awareness to the whole.

Without employing your analytic mind or applying words or language, try to feel what the birds are saying. This is language beyond words – bird language. Can you feel their communication? It is wonderful, isn't it?

CHAPTER 31

LIVING ON THE TIDE

(BEYOND TECHNIQUE)

This book is based on a course I have been teaching for more than ten years. The course is practical and sensory, so it has been interesting to format it into a book. It has allowed me to explain in more detail how my approach has developed.

We have been on a journey of discovery. The journey started with simple, basic processes and, by the end, we have looked at complex sensory practices. On our journey, we have learnt many techniques and practices, each of which builds on the perceptual understanding of the last. Without the foundational practices, the latter stages are impossible. Learning here involves a sensory change – literally, a change in perception and even consciousness. Then, changes become embodied and have a lasting effect.

We started with learning about the idea of neutral, the process of taking our mind out of gear so that our being can return to a more childlike state, not driven ever forwards by our will. To achieve this, we actively brought ourselves into contact with our immediate thoughts, feelings and emotions, and we learnt to accept, allow and, finally, observe them without judgement.

From here, we looked at the ideas of timing and tempo, and the gift of the present. We also looked at sitting posture and the importance of developing a practice. In the process, we learnt to become aware of a natural timing and flow. Then we explored the wonderful experience of learning to sense the great stillness that is always present and lies behind all activity. We started to develop a living relationship with this stillness and to gain awareness of our attention, looking at where it is in time and space. We then explored the process of giving something our full and pure attention, and the benefits of this. From here, we turned our attention to ourselves and learnt techniques to start to feel fluidity within our body, and to let that fluidity manifest so that eventually we feel as though we are a fluid body.

With this new knowledge about fluidity, we looked at some of the great indigenous tribes of the world and the connection they felt with the wind.

We next studied the idea that within this fluidity there is a motion, a slow, breathing, fluid motion we could call the great tide or the long tide. We went on to practise feeling it, learning to take our awareness to the stillness, and waiting until motion arises from stillness.

Next, we started on an exploration of our senses – how we use them and how we have programmed them. The course has been about developing sensory awareness, meaning developing our senses, so first we had to understand a little of how they function. With each technique we were deepening our sensory understanding of neutral and stillness – both inside and outside of ourselves – and of motion, notably when and where it arises from stillness. We went on to concentrate our awareness at that place in our sensory field where motion arises, and learnt to keep our attention there and wait to see what happens.

Fulcrums were explored in the next phase. This served the purpose of allowing us to be aware of exactly where our attention lies in each moment. From here, we started to look at the important process of changing our attention from whatever in our body feels blocked, unhappy or ill at ease to whatever feels sweet, light and fluid. This was first explored by the idea of directing our breathing into areas of our body in the form of soft and releasing breaths. It started us on the process of connecting to the potential for health within our bodies. This was followed up by an exploration of the fire of ignition, the practice of engaging with the animating potency within us.

Next, we started to explore and practise the idea and sense of dynamic stillness, which is the stillness that contains the potential for all motion. This brought specific sensory changes, which we explored in detail. From here, we developed the idea of meeting our health to learn a practice of self-healing.

We then introduced the idea and experience of wholeness and how that potentially meets oneness. This led us into an exploration of sensing nature and the practice of developing a holistic felt-sense and, through it, how we can gain deep insights into nature.

These processes have, I hope, started us on a path to deepen our self-awareness and self-acceptance. They have expanded our sensory awareness, deepened our connection to stillness and dynamic stillness, the tide and nature, and changed our relationship to our health. But what about in normal daily life? What if we are deeply worried about someone close, a job situation or finances and feel extremely stressed? Can any of this be helpful if all we can think about is something that is a very real worry? Is it possible, through all this practice, to live in stillness, connection and health regardless?

The first step is to practise the accept, allow and observe process, and just let the stress be the stress – it's OK. Then we can employ one or two of the many techniques we have explored to change our reaction to the stress. It does not remove the stress, but it helps change the way we react to it and deal with it.

But how can we practise in everyday life? When I do my daily practice I exercise for twenty minutes then sit down and practice some elements we have explored here, always a little differently.

This Dynamics of Stillness practice is a little different from meditation because it involves sensory awareness, felt-sense and allowing our attention to move, either through our own volition or by the tide or the moment.

My goal for my daily practice often changes. It can be to sense nature deeply, to feel the tide, to feel stillness or to do a little self-healing. Whatever I do on any given day, it is all practice. I use what I call 'ways into stillness', which I always vary. I start with one of the following: softness of breath, sensing the stillness, waiting for the tide, or practising acceptance and observing whatever I am feeling. What I am attuned to is the developing, proliferating stillness and, eventually, to dynamic stillness. I tend to use more than one technique; I just go with what works on the day and in the moment – each time will be different. I will use any of the techniques covered in our practices and often move freely between them until I reach a good state of neutral and then let the stillness or the great tide come or the dynamic stillness.

I try to allow my mind to be moved by the moment – to always allow and never to fix it. I like to get a deep sense of stillness within me and around me. Each time we feel the stillness, tide or dynamic stillness, our relationship deepens with them and we are able to gain more from our practice.

When dynamic stillness arrives, it brings a state of 'no-mind', almost an emptiness where I lose time and space for a while. This can last for ten minutes or much longer, but, eventually, my attention returns. With a holistic felt-sense, I may concentrate for a while on a process of unwinding, or of feeling warmth in my body, or a feeling of the tide arriving, or birdsong or the wind. Often, though, I am left with a thought or feeling about something to write or do. It is usually something that has resolved itself in my mind without me actively thinking about it at all. I trust this sense as I feel it comes from somewhere deep within me. What is nice is to take two things with me into the day:

The first is an awareness of the underlying stillness that is behind everything. If I try to check in with this awareness during the day, then my day feels peaceful and more enjoyable.

The other thing I take with me into the day is being aware of a sense of when motion arises from the stillness, or a sense of when the great tide moves through me. This feels deeply healing and connecting.

These practices could help bring us closer to what the Taoists call 'being with the Tao', or being moved by life. Again, the more I do it, the more I *can* do it. Practice really does make

these perceptual processes come alive. Throughout the day, I like to use my felt-sense to connect with nature whenever I can – I just really enjoy it. I think we can all develop our own practice that works best for us.

I really hope you enjoy these practices. They have been deeply enriching for me, so much so that I wanted to share what I have spent years working on and learning.

PRACTICE 31

Beyond Technique

At this stage, you should be able to practise whether you are standing, sitting, on a train or anywhere really. You should be able to do this in nature, alone or even in a crowded room.

By now, you do not need step-by-step instructions. Instead, let your attention focus on some developing sensations while being moved by the moment. Sense stillness and motion.

Start with the process of allowing, accepting and then observing all thoughts, feelings and emotions – whether they be good or bad. At the same time, let your attention fall onto whatever comes up. This could be the stillness all around you, or a sense of something that feels soft, delicate or fluid in your body, or the feeling of motion of the great tide as it arises from stillness.

Try to let your attention be moved by whatever comes up during your practice, but always allow your attention to come back to the proliferating stillness in and around you.

Be aware, also, of the softening, opening and calming process within you. Allow all this to happen at the same time, without fixing your attention on anything in particular.

When your attention softens itself into dynamic stillness, just go with that process and be taken by it. There is no technique but a deepening dynamic stillness.

INDEX

I owe a huge debt of gratitude to my teachers over the last 30 years. The osteopaths, both living and passed, include Dr Andrew Taylor Still, Dr Will Sutherland, Dr Edna Lay, Dr Anne Wales, Dr Rollin Becker, Stuart Korth and Dr Jim Jealous.

My greatest teachers, though, are my patients, especially those special children who never fail to amaze me. Each day I learn a little more and deepen my understanding and love of life through my practice.

This book has also been influenced by a lifetime of study of Taoism, especially the works of the Complete Reality Schools, which I am greatly indebted. There are also threads within this work influenced by various schools of Buddhism. Other threads of influence come from the words of Johann Wolfgang von Goethe and the spiritual practices of Rudolf Steiner.

The nature connection of some of the indigenous world tribes have strongly influenced my practice, including the Bushmen of the Kalahari through the words of Laurens van de Post and the Guatamalan Mayans who I had the good fortune to live with and learn from for 6 months in the late 1990s.

To my great friend and colleague Mary Bollingbroke – we learnt how to sense the natural world together, both within our patients and the world around us.

To my wonderful three children Lou, Mia and Dylan, who continue daily to open my heart with love.

Lastly, to my wife Mara – my partner, my life.

Course information

Ian Wright runs two courses on to the Dynamics of Stillness in a variety of locations. Visit thedynamicsofstillness.com for more information. This website also provides a free series of downloadable podcasts that give an introduction to meditation.

Picture Credits:

Shutterstockphoto.Inc Elena Ray

Eddison Books Limited
Managing Director Lisa Dyer
Managing Editor Nicolette Kaponis
Editor Zia Mattocks

Proofreader Jane Donovan
Indexer Angie Hipkin
Design Roger Walton Studio
Production Gary Hayes